THE LITERARY TEMPER
OF
THE ENGLISH PURITANS

by

LAWRENCE A. SASEK

GREENWOOD PRESS, PUBLISHERS
NEW YORK

Copyright © 1961 by Louisiana State University Press

Reprinted by permission
of Louisiana State University Press

First Greenwood Reprinting 1969

Library of Congress Catalogue Card Number 78-88936

SBN 8371-2333-X

PRINTED IN UNITED STATES OF AMERICA

For Gloria

Preface

SEVERAL YEARS AGO, while studying the literary milieu of *Paradise Lost*, I attempted to find out how the English puritans received and interpreted classical epic. Since studies of puritanism did not furnish a conclusive answer, I decided to investigate the problem myself. I soon discovered that the answer could be found only implicitly, and then in a study of the puritan attitude toward secular literary art in general. In time I found also that no definite conclusions were possible, but the evidence seemed valuable and I continued until I felt justified in assuming I could discover no further variety of comment. I remain acutely, uncomfortably aware of all that I have not done—that I have not defined puritan literary theory, for instance—yet I hope that what I have done will have some value, that this study will reveal a pattern of comments useful to the advancement of knowledge of the puritans' influence on the literary temper of their time.

Throughout this study I have assumed the editorial function of modernizing spelling and, where clarity could be served, punctuation. I could see no purpose in literal transcription of texts I have used solely because of their content, not their style.

It is a pleasure to acknowledge my gratitude for the assistance I have received from the beginning of this project to its completion. The staffs of the Reading Room of the British Museum, the Harvard University Library, and the Louisiana State University Library extended to me their traditional courtesy. From the Research Council of Louisiana State University I received a grant to help complete the study. Professor Waldo F. McNeir, the editor of the Humanities Series of the Louisiana State University Studies, gave advice and editorial assistance beyond the call of duty. The profit I have received from the criticism of my readers, Professor William Haller of the Folger Shakespeare Library and Professors Perry Miller and Kenneth Murdock of Harvard University, has been limited only by my capacity to follow their generous advice. Finally, it would be presumptuous to try to describe the full extent of my debt to my wife for her constant encouragement. Of course, the responsibility for whatever errors and shortcomings remain in this study is entirely my own.

L. A. S.

Contents

CHAPTER 1

Introduction

As STUDIES of puritanism in England and America increase in number and illuminate obscure byroads as well as the main roads of puritan endeavor and thought, the role of the puritans in literary history should become clearer, more sharply defined. Yet, chief among the things sharpened are the horns of a dilemma that confronts the student of literature. When he tries to visualize the puritan, especially the puritan of Old England, he gradually realizes two contrasting images, unreconcilable except perhaps in a Jekyll and Hyde fantasy. On the one hand, in literary studies, the puritan looms forth in the garb and with the attitude of Malvolio or Zeal of the Land Busy. By contrast, in special studies of puritanism, the typical representative of the movement invariably resembles a lesser Milton, or more erudite Bunyan.

In histories of seventeenth-century English literature, the puritans usually are given significant but invidious mention. Their influence upon the literary arts is considered important, but negative, even destructive. Occasionally references are made to a puritan humanist or to puritan love of music, but most frequently the puritan appears as an enemy of the very spirit of art, much less amiable, because of his strict, often hypocritical, denunciation of the sensuous, than the most libidinous and wayward cavalier, whose vices are easily redeemed, for students of literature, by his contributions to lyric poetry. Contrasted with the Anglican, the puritan is again the destroyer; while the former defends a native tradition, including a humanistic accommodation between worldly art and the pre-eminent other-worldly concerns of religion, the latter intolerantly and narrowly tries to root out of the religious tradition all its sensuous beauty and, consequently, much of its humanity, to transform it into an unlovely and forbidding doctrine that few men would wish to live by. At worst, literary historians who tend to look upon the puritans solely as enemies of the vital art of their time have an attitude similar, perhaps, to that of the modern stereotype of the professor of Greek who contemns Faulkner and Hemingway without reading them.

What might be called the literary concept of the puritan is supported by a number of historical facts. Shakespeare, Jonson, and other poets and dramatists looked upon the puritans as enemies. In 1642 the theatres were closed by an act of Parliament, and the most productive era of English dramatic history came to an end. During the mid-seventeenth century the rich tradition of the Renaissance lyric was almost completely spent. The lyric impulse itself was so weakened that satire became the dominant mode of poetic expression for about a century. The opulence of baroque prose gave way to a style relatively poor in metaphor, connotativeness, and rhythmic complexity, a style more lucid, but more bare and simple. For these phenomena the puritans are made to bear much of the responsibility. The parliament that closed the theatres was dominated by them and influenced by their unremitting attacks on the stage. The lyric impulse was weakened, we are told, by the incessant battering of puritan insistence upon the didactic aim of literature, an insistence that concommitantly fostered the growth of satire. The metaphors and sensuous periods of Donne and Browne fell before the puritan demand for a prose style simple enough for the most uneducated Christian to understand. Much of the responsibility for the changes in prose style is shared by the Royal Society and the rest of the Baconian movement, which turned men's concerns from beauty to utility; but somehow puritanism seems less positive and fruitful, less a means to a laudable end, and more a reprehensible exaltation of asceticism for its own sake, than does the burgeoning science.

The lack of artistic achievement among the puritans reinforces the notion that they were unsympathetic critics, if not enemies, of literature. When we examine the writings of a movement that was directed by many of the finest intellects of nearly a century of English history, we find only two indisputably excellent literary artists, Milton and Bunyan, neither of whom can redeem puritanism artistically. Bunyan is easily discounted because of his extremely narrow range in style and subject, and Milton, because of his striking individuality, cannot be called representative. In every literary school, the greater writers merely overshadow related figures of lesser ability, their predecessors, contemporaries, followers, and imitators within the tradition; their works are at the top of a gradually ascending scale of merit; for instance, Shakespeare appears in Elizabethan drama as a mountain surrounded by numerous lower peaks and foothills. But Milton stands alone among the puritans. Inevitably we ask if Milton is not a great artist in spite of his puritanism, if the individuality of his contribution to literature does not arise from a unique blend of Renaissance humanism and puritanism, a blend of elements so conflicting that it could be achieved only by the most extraordinary genius. Whatever the reason, Milton, of all English writers, is *sui generis*, and his example can prove nothing about his religious, intellectual, and political allies.

Sympathetic studies of puritans—and practically all the thorough, scholarly studies are sympathetic—present a vastly more amiable picture, although they have not yet exorcised the Malvolio-like spectre that haunts literary history. William Haller, Perry Miller, Kenneth Murdock, and Samuel Eliot Morison have shown conclusively that puritanism and humanism were not mutually exclusive, not even mutually repugnant, and that puritans studied and taught the classics, wrote voluminously in a number of traditional literary forms, and tuned sensitive ears to the charms of verse and prose style, both classical and vernacular.[1] The typical representative of the movement for a more

---

[1] William Haller, *The Rise of Puritanism* (New York: Columbia University Press, 1938), and *Liberty and Reformation in the Puritan Revolution* (New York: Columbia University Press, 1955); Perry Miller, *The New England Mind: The Seventeenth Century* (New York: The MacMillan Company, 1939); Kenneth B. Murdock, *Literature and Theology in Colonial*

thorough reformation in Old England and the typical guardian
of the ancestral culture in New England bear little resemblance
to the typical enemy of the poets and playwrights.

In fact they are not identical. The difference in characterization can be explained largely by differences in emphasis, and
by the tendency of scholars in one group to accept at face value
the polemic characterization of the embattled dramatist whom
they study sympathetically, in contrast with the tendency of
scholars of another group to project throughout puritanism the
personalities they have discovered in their probing of the mind
and temper of Richard Baxter and Richard Sibbes. Finally, the
difference becomes thoroughly understandable when one un-
covers the definitions of puritanism implicit and explicit in the
comments on the puritan.

The term *puritan* is in fact defined in several conflicting ways,
and often the definition in itself explains subsequent attitudes
towards the puritans and their effect on literature. The semantic
obscurity in which it is involved is not of modern origin, for
puritan was in its inception an ambivalent or, at least, confusing
term. The sixteenth-century religious groups first stigmatized
by it protested honestly and with apparently unconscious irrele-
vance that they loathed the ancient *Catharoi* as much as did
their opponents. As the term came to be used more recklessly
and indiscriminately, and applied to more generally respectable
churchmen, many adopted it and wore it proudly, but not without making distinctions which testify to its comprehensiveness
and vagueness. Robert Bolton, for example, defined and rejected
nine religious groups and attitudes which were given the name
puritan before he embraced a tenth and, in his opinion, correct
definition.[2]

New England (Cambridge, Mass.: Harvard University Press, 1949) ; Samuel
Eliot Morison, *The Intellectual Life of Colonial New England* (New York:
New York University Press, 1956) .

[2]Robert Bolton, *Two Sermons Preached at Northampton* (1635) , 83-88. For
a representative sampling of sixteenth- and seventeenth-century definitions
of puritanism, see H. Hensley Hensen, *Puritanism in England* (London:
Hodder and Stoughton, 1912) , 6 ff. G. P. Gooch has pointed out that whereas
Parliament in 1605 had "expressly disowned" the name *puritan*, Pym in 1625
declared that it covered "the greatest part of the King's true subjects." Gooch,

The confusion that the word has brought into modern literary studies can be illustrated by the pioneering and still valuable work of E. N. S. Thompson, *The Controversy between the Puritans and the Stage* (New York: Henry Holt and Co., 1903).[3] Its major shortcoming, a tendency to equate puritanism with dislike of the theatre, is reflected by random comments on the puritans in literary studies not concerned directly with the movement. In fact, the implied definition of *puritan* is often "one who attacked the stage" (or "poetry" or "art"), and the vehemence of the attack becomes a measure of the degree of puritan sympathy. Thus the word *puritan* becomes redundant, or at best a convenient term for a kind of ascetic moral rigor. Such word usage seems plausible enough, and allows the author to progress smoothly enough through his chosen field; but the student who follows him and then passes on into ecclesiastical history very likely runs head on into a contradicting and more solidly established definition, built up by centuries of study of the puritan movement. He finds the term has a more clearly and solidly established meaning in ecclesiastical history, and the definitions often conflict. A "puritan" opponent of the stage may be an orthodox Anglican who fought the puritans and, conversely, an active puritan opponent of the established church can, in literary history, turn out to be quite unpuritanical. For instance, George Herbert, the loyal Anglican, was more "puritan" in literary temper than Andrew Marvell, the civil servant of the puritan government, or Andrew May, the man who aspired to be poet laureate of the puritan party. The literary definition thus creates graver problems than it solves, and it tells us nothing of the literary attitudes of the people who have long been designated puritans by students of the religious and political history of the sixteenth and seventeenth centuries.[4]

English Democratic Ideas in the Seventeenth Century (2d ed., New York: Harper and Brothers, 1959), 60. (In all citations of sixteenth- and seventeenth-century texts, the place of publication is London, unless it is otherwise indicated.)

[3]For instance, Charles Cullen, "Puritanism and the Stage," *Proceedings of the Royal Philosophical Society of Glasgow*, XLIII (1911-1912), 153-81, and T. S. Graves, "Puritanism and the Stage," *Studies in Philology*, XVIII (1921), 141-69.

[4]For example, Allan Holaday, "Giles Fletcher and the Puritans," *Journal*

An important question is whether the term *puritan* can have any meaning in literary history other than the loose one given it. In other words, did the puritans, as defined by other historians, have a distinct literary theory, or perhaps a literary attitude based on an implicit theory? Many studies of seventeenth-century literature and thought indicate that they did. For instance, Professor Miller, in numerous references to the "puritan aesthetic," clearly assumes that the literary theory of the puritans can be defined, but he deals primarily with the New England colonists, a relatively homogeneous group in spite of their frequent disagreements. Professor Murdock defines a puritan literary attitude as it existed in New England and cites English writers in illustration of his thesis.[5] Patrick Cruttwell, in *The Shakespearean Moment*, distinguishes puritan from non-puritan objections to plays and other forms of art by their tone, and traces the differences to philosophic and religious attitudes. In effect, he makes the puritan the true ascetic; but he distinguishes puritan asceticism by kind, not merely by degree, and relates it to nonliterary defining characteristics of puritanism. Yet his discussion of puritanism is incidental, and his critical remarks, though significant, seem to call for documentation and qualification.[6]

The validity of any study of puritan attitudes toward literature presupposes a reasonably clear definition of the movement, and perhaps the ambiguity of some current definitions has caused literary scholars to ignore them and to develop a substitute out of literary history alone. Certainly many of the definitions are not congruent; but, as often happens, the widest divergences appear between the more rigid and specific definitions, particularly between those which try to identify the essential

of English and Germanic Philology, LIV (1955), 578-86, notes that Fletcher is Anglican in "theology" but puritan in his attitude toward the theatre, and questions the relative meanings of the two terms. A concise yet detailed summary of the changing issues in the conflict is given in "The Evolving Pattern of Religious Dispute," the first chapter of William P. Holden, *Anti-Puritan Satire 1572-1642* (New Haven: Yale University Press, 1954).

[5]*Literature and Theology*, 31 ff.

[6]Patrick Cruttwell, *The Shakespearean Moment* (New York: Columbia University Press, 1955), 160-61.

beliefs or peculiar characteristics of the puritan ethic and theology. Scholars who disagree on the essence of the movement yet agree as well as necessary on the area it included. And for this study, an adequate working definition need only identify specific writers of the sixteenth and seventeenth centuries as puritans.

The general, conservative definition seems adequate; one need merely say that the puritans were the people who insisted on a more stringent reform of the English church than the authorities of the establishment would allow. Avoiding doubtful cases, one may locate the beginning of the movement with Thomas Cartwright and his contemporaries and its end with Baxter.[7] The specific points of contention changed with time; from protests directed most frequently against church vestments and ritual under Elizabeth, the puritans went on to opposition to Arminianism under James, and to a frontal attack upon the Anglican establishment itself under Charles, an attack that, after spectacular but temporary success, dwindled into defensive opposition, like Baxter's, to the church of the Restoration. The movement was not unified. by any one doctrine or code of belief; the interminable debates and eventual failure of the Westminster Assembly and the breaking up of the puritan movement into antagonistic, warring factions after victory had been achieved over the bishops indicate its religious heterogeneity clearly enough. The degrees of church reform sought by various groups also differed widely, from the aims of the Presbyterians, who insisted on stopping with a new kind of establishment, to those of the Quakers, who recognized no professional ministry. After 1642 the term "puritanism" becomes impossible to define as a belief or body of principles,[8] but it would cause much the same trouble during the reign of James I. The term is most useful if we apply it to the great force opposing the established church, the force that gave religious character and ideals to one of the opposing sides in the Civil War, that helped sus-

---

[7]The terms of the definition are used by Hugh Martin, *Puritanism and Richard Baxter* (London: SCM Press, Ltd., 1954) , 46.

[8]See Charles H. George, "A Social Interpretation of English Puritanism," *Journal of Modern History*, XXV (1953) , 327-42.

tain the Commonwealth, and that was dissipated at the Restoration, but yet had enough residual vitality to force the settlement of 1688.[9] Whether the question of the moment was ritual, doctrine, or church government, the puritan was the man who opposed the Anglican by demanding a more drastic change from Roman Catholicism, a more thorough reformation, than the established church felt it could permit. With qualifications, this definition applies also to the era when the bishops had no effective power; for Anglican sentiment persisted, and even in their triumph, in spite of their internal, fragmenting strife, the puritans were to a degree unified by hatred of the old order and fear of its possible return.

Since the working definition of a puritan is based on a religious, even a specifically ecclesiastical, attitude, the writers easiest to identify as puritans are the ministers and others who wrote about religion. This fact presents a major obstacle to the study of puritan literary attitudes. The ministers wrote voluminously, but literature as an art was not their primary concern. Except for attacks on the stage, their comments on literary topics are random and incidental. One is confronted by a vast mass of writings from which he must extract brief, inconclusive, and often indirect statements. These in turn must be interpreted in their context and according to the immediate purpose of the writer. Completeness is hardly possible; the best one can hope is to achieve a representative sampling of puritan statements on literature, and from it to derive a general picture, with vague and blurred edges but perhaps a distinct central focus, of a pattern of attitudes.

The objection may be raised that in a study of literary attitudes, the writings of ministers are less important than those of poets, and puritanism did have its poets, though few deserve mention in a literary history of reasonable brevity and selectivity. But one may as well object on principle to a study of the literary impact of an extraliterary movement. In answer, one

---

[9]As Holden says, "The core of the argument to 1642 is beyond question religious" (*Anti-Puritan Satire*, ix); and surely nearly everyone would grant that religious issues were basic in the controversies of the Civil War and Interregnum.

need only say that as long as the word "puritan" is used in literary histories, this kind of study is necessary. Moreover, the ministers were the intellectual and spiritual leaders of puritanism; their attitudes towards literature, among other things, conditioned its reception among the public under their spiritual tutelage. The poets were largely followers, putting into effect with more or less consistency the attitudes explicit and implicit in the teachings of the religious leaders, and few of them left any relevant comments on their art. Again the one outstanding exception is Milton, but because Milton is an exception in so many ways, the question with which he is most fruitfully approached is not "What can we learn of puritanism from Milton?" but "How do Milton's beliefs agree with those of the puritans in general?" And that is another and subsequent question.

In a study such as this, the commonplace statement is even more important than the original and unique. The latter may establish the boundaries of opinion and illustrate the range of individual variations, but the former, more importantly, gives the ideas that were reiterated and inculcated until they affected the response of the general public. To some extent the importance of commonplaces makes up for the lack of exhaustive study of all possible sources. Even though hampered by unavailability of texts, one can achieve a representative sampling, and one large enough to demonstrate which ideas and tendencies were the most common and influential. One can establish a norm, or a pattern of variations, or, sometimes, a pattern of contradictions

Perhaps the reader should be given several further cautions. The following chapters do not constitute a study of the puritan mind; consequently, they do not seek to define a literary theory in the classic sense of the term. For instance, the relative influence of Aristotelian and Platonic theories of rhetoric and poetry will not be explored. The study has a more limited aim, to outline the puritans' opinions on various topics that are significant for an estimate of their impact upon the literature of their time. The outline derived is in few places a rigid pattern, and often it is unsymmetrical; for the variety of attitudes would allow systematic classification only at the expense of distortion. On

some points exploration seems more valuable than attempts
at definition, for instead of the concise, definite principles one
would like to present, only broad and highly qualified generali-
zations are possible. Frequently, also, puritan comments differ
only in tone, and then slightly. from the commonplaces of
Renaissance literary criticism. But where no coherent or dis-
tinctive puritan attitude can be isolated, that fact should be
worth noting and substantiating, in view of the regularity with
which inflexible theories are ascribed to the puritans. Moreover,
even general descriptive statements, and even documentation of
more or less accepted statements, about the literary temper of
the puritans may help to correct some misapprehensions and to
fill a gap in our knowledge of the literary character of the late
sixteenth and early seventeenth centuries.

CHAPTER 2

The Groaning Press

LITERATURE, in the most comprehensive sense of the term, did not suffer during the era of puritan ascendancy. While actors were thrown out of work, printers and booksellers flourished. Although they believed and insisted vehemently that the Bible was the one book necessary to salvation, the puritan ministers continued to fill the bookshops with works of their own. As Haller summarizes, and explains, the paradoxical situation, "Nothing did more to foster the production of books than the enormous literature of edification, comment, and controversy that the Bible evoked." [1] Today any relevant bibliography gives evidence of the vast quantity of writing, from theological treatises to sermons, devotional works, and controversial pamphlets, that puritanism has bequeathed to modern libraries. A consecutive reading of Brook's *Lives of the Puritans* gives the impression that nearly every minister was an author, and many of the "lives" seem to be substantially bibliographies of the subjects' publications.

The Bible, of course, needed interpretation, commentary, and application to immediate problems. Its sufficiency did not make auxiliary writings redundant, and its style—its imagery, parables, terse and conflicting statements—encouraged them. But another basic tenet of puritanism did give pause to the ministers and necessitated some justification of and apology for their writings. Haller has documented the puritan regard for preaching, the

---

[1]Haller, *Liberty and Reformation in the Puritan Revolution*, 139.

belief common to the whole movement, in "a godly, preaching ministry." [2]

The puritans were concerned, of course, for the welfare of the illiterate. But contemporary psychology also gave a prime importance to spoken discourse. Regeneration could be achieved only by a moving of the spirit—by working upon the emotions—and the majority apparently felt that auditory impressions were more basic and pervasive than visual ones. Peter Smith argues against a minority view by rejecting Horace's theory that "things move more dully by the ear than by the eye," countering with Romans 10:17, "The Apostle saith of faith, 'It comes by hearing.' " [3] Even ministers who did not explore the psychology of St. Paul's statement, or even repeat it, yet apparently took it as an axiom.

The logic and intensity of the argument for preaching that was erected upon this belief can be illustrated by Arthur Dent. In the work immortalized by Bunyan's tribute, *The Plain Man's Pathway to Heaven*, the argument runs, "If we will have heaven, we must have Christ. If we will have Christ, we must have faith. If we will have faith, we must have the word preached. Then it followeth thus: if we will have heaven we must have the word preached. Then I conclude that preaching generally, and for the most part, is of absolute necessity unto eternal life." [4] The very redundancy breathes conviction. Logically, any minister who devoted time to writing was open to the charge that he was neglecting his duty. Even the publication of a sermon involved some time for revision, as numerous prefaces testify. And the reading of books might seem to the faithful a substitute for the hearing of sermons.

That the charge was often made, or at least very often antici-

---

[2]*Ibid.*, 3-31.

[3]Peter Smith, *A Sermon Preached before . . . Commons . . . May 29, 1644* (1644), ep. ded. The basis of puritan literary theory in puritan psychology is explained by Murdock in *Literature and Theology*, especially in Chapter 2, "The Puritan Literary Attitude." (A more general designation of the source of a citation is given wherever the page number or signature is missing, or wherever the signature does not seem very helpful in locating the exact page.)

[4]Arthur Dent, *The Plaine Mans Pathway to Heaven* (1625), 336-37.

pated, is clear enough from the large number of apologetic
prefaces, letters to readers, and dedicatory epistles in which the
puritan authors try to justify writing and publication. From
such apologies one cannot gain any insight into a literary theory
in the classical sense of the term, but he can get a notion of the
puritan attitude toward the function and efficacy of the written
word, an attitude that certainly had implications for all literature.

Many of the puritans faced directly the problem of the relative importance of preaching and writing in an attempt to justify,
at least as a subordinate activity, their neglect of the pulpit for
the study. For some, a liberal definition of preaching justified
the writing ministry. In a preface to Sibbes's *Exposition of II
Corinthians iv*, Simeon Ashe, James Nalton, and Joseph Church
declared that "there are three ways by which a minister preaches:
by doctrine, life, and writing." [5] The implication is that all are
of equal importance, unless the emphasis on the difficulty of
leading an exemplary life—"It is easier to preach twenty sermons
than to mortify one lust"—gives pre-eminence to teaching by example. Definitely implied here is a justification of publishing
biographies, even autobiographies, of the puritan saints. The
general acceptance of this attitude is evident in the popularity
and high reputation of Fox's *Acts and Monuments* and, later,
Samuel Clarke's *Lives of Sundry Eminent Persons* and *Mar-
tyrology*. The same belief in the three types of preaching is expressed in many other prefaces, notably in Edward Leigh's praise
of William Whately, the famed Banbury preacher, who provided
an example of all three. Whately is called "an example and pattern of all good works"; a learned writer, a scholar who knew
Hebrew, Greek, logic, philosophy, rhetoric, and oratory, "as his
printed treatises abundantly testify"; and a master of elocution,
who "had words at will and could readily and aptly express
himself in his sermons." [6]

---

[5] *The Complete Works of Richard Sibbes*, ed. A. B. Grosart (7 vols., Edin-
burgh, 1862-64), IV, 309. Unless chronology is significant, puritan statements are treated as though they were contemporaneous. This approach
has good precedent, and it seems perfectly logical where opinions show
little change with time.

[6] William Whately, *Prototypes* (1647), sig. A4.

But Whately himself, demonstrating that puritan opinion was varied, believed that preaching was more effective, and hence more valuable, than writing: "Without question the word preached is more powerfully effectual to regeneration than the word read." [7] Whately is, of course, arguing against Anglican overemphasis—as the puritans saw it—on reading in the church service, but his insistence on preaching from the pulpit seems absolute. The reasons for the greater efficacy of the word preached are given by many others. Samuel Hieron states his reason very simply: "The matter cannot be so lively from the pen as from the tongue." [8] Both Whately and Hieron were noted chiefly as preachers, but the same idea is expressed in very similar terms by the scholarly Thomas Gataker, whose interests were divided between the ministry and critical studies of the classics: "The lifeless letter, for vivacity and efficacy, cometh far short of the living voice." [9] The contrast between life and death is stark enough to make one suspect Gataker of overstating one side of a controversial issue, but he makes the same point elsewhere, calling elocution "not the prime part only of oratory, but, in effect, *all in all*, and the sum of all." [10] Both *oratory* and *elocution* (style) were terms applied by Renaissance theorists to written discourse; yet the terms retained something of their original, root sense.

Gataker, however, did not deny all value to writing, as the bibliography of his works testifies. His theory is consistent with his practice in giving writing an important function: "By it we may speak as well to the absent as to the present." [11] A similar function was attributed to books by the London preacher, William Gouge, who noted they can disseminate the minister's word more widely in both time and space, sending it to remote places and preserving it for future generations. Gouge considers preaching "the principal part" of his function, nevertheless, because it can "work upon the affections." Writing, by contrast, is

---

[7] Whately, *The New Birth* (1618), 18-19.
[8] *The Works of Mr. Sam. Hieron* (1634-35), ep. ded. to *Three Sermons*.
[9] Thomas Gataker, *Certain Sermons* (1637), 28.
[10] *Ibid.*, 308.
[11] *Ibid.*

designed "to inform the judgment," [12] a subordinate function because, like most of his contemporaries, Gouge believed that regeneration was primarily a psychological process. But, in general, the wider dissemination of the written word was the one advantage granted writing by those most insistent on the greater efficacy of preaching; and Gouge himself lists it as the only one in a preface to the works of Thomas Taylor, a preface signed by eleven others as well. [13] In specific cases other considerations were urged. Henry Smith excused his writing, on one occasion, by pleading an illness that kept him from preaching, as did Edward Reynolds. [14] But as important as the reasons themselves is the fact that reasons were given, often apologetically. For many puritans, writing had to be excused, even when considered a subordinate activity.

The tone of the excuses is also important, however. Often they are so eloquent or insistent that one suspects many puritans believed that writing was, in the long run, more efficacious, that a written sermon or treatise might more effectively promote the work of salvation than a sermon preached before a congregation. An apology may be one-sided, of course, and all the apologies were addressed to readers largely convinced of the need for preaching; but the very fact that preaching was a *sine qua non* of salvation and its need practically an article of faith with the puritans gives significance to the attempts to equate writing with it, or to give writing greater importance. Moreover, the puritans would not casually depreciate an activity that distinguished them from their opponents. Writing thus gets high praise when Sibbes, in a preface to a sermon by Gataker, implies that its wider audience more or less compensates for the "deeper impressions" made by preaching. [15] Likewise, the seemingly offhand remark by William Greenhill, "A word spoken is soon

---

[12] *The Works of William Gouge* (2 vols., 1627), I, sig. A5v. The psychology of regeneration has been explained by Haller, *Rise of Puritanism*, 128-72, and Miller, *New England Mind*, 280-330.

[13] *The Works of . . . Dr. Thom. Taylor* (1653), preface.

[14] *The Sermons of Mr. Henry Smith* (1675), preface; *The Whole Works of the Right Rev. Edward Reynolds*, ed. Alexander Chalmers (6 vols., London, 1826), III, 171.

[15] Sibbes, *Works*, VII, 561.

forgotten, but what is written remains, and may do you, your children, and your children's children good," [16] in view of its implications, must have been written advisedly. Again, Peter Smith, after insisting that hearing comes by faith, admitted that "memory is frail" and that it was useful to read what one had heard. [17] Both Sibbes and Greenhill were praising the works of writers, and Smith was justifying the publication of his sermon, but all were noted preachers who would not casually elevate writing to the high level of esteem occupied by their chief function.

Brief comments gain significance when paralleled by lengthy arguments of the same import; and the more detailed discussion of the same question by Richard Baxter shows that Greenhill and Sibbes were affirming a position that others were ready to justify at length. Traditionally, Baxter considers writing a form of preaching, calling books, "domestic, present, constant, judicious, pertinent, yea, and powerful sermons." Traditionally, also, he ascribes to "vocal preaching" an advantage in "moving the affections." On the same side, he adduces the less common but equally substantial argument that preaching can be "diversified according to the state of the congregation," or suited to the audience. But the advantages of books seem more numerous, if not more weighty. One can discount his argument that, unlike preachers, books cannot be silenced, as a personal, topical utterance, applicable chiefly during the Restoration and made more vehement by Baxter's immediate experience than its substance may warrant. But his other comments are judiciously and factually stated: through books one can often hear better preachers than his own minister; books are less expensive than ministers; books can be chosen by the individual according to his need; books are available at any time; books can be memorized. In the manner of puritan controversialists, Baxter finds justification for his argument in the Bible: "The Holy Ghost chose the way of writing to preserve His doctrines and laws." [18] His example may be logically irrelevant, but it shows vividly how the Bible, far from supplanting all other books,

---

[16] *The Works of the Rev. William Bridge* (5 vols., London, 1845), I, 297.
[17] Peter Smith, *Sermon Preached before Commons*, ep. ded.
[18] Richard Baxter, *A Christian Directory* (1673), 60.

not only became a stimulus to further writing and publication, but even a justification of writing.

Easiest to defend were posthumous publications. Here the writer himself did not have to account for the time spent on his writing, and the publisher could argue the almost self-evident utility of preserving the dead man's words and extending his audience to include posterity. The Biblical text most popular with literary executors was a portion of Hebrews 11:4: "he being dead yet speaketh." The Biblical context had no relevance, but the phrase was used as a slogan, not as an argument. And it appears frequently enough; not only were books reprinted, or published in collected editions, but many, like those of Sibbes, were printed from manuscripts for the first time, when the author had become a legend or an object of puritan hagiolatry. Thomas Manton, in a preface to Sibbes's commentary on II Corinthians 1, testifies to the large number of edifying works published only after their authors were dead, remarking that "not only the life, but the death of God's servants hath been profitable to his church, by that means many useful treatises being freed from the privacy and obscureness to which, by modesty of the author, they were formerly confined." Manton suggests other possible reasons, besides modesty, for the reluctance to publish, including a desire to emulate Christ and fear of adverse criticism of their works. He does not suggest that God's servants did not believe in writing. Sibbes, as we have seen, gave it an important function, and Manton notes that many of his works were corrected and revised for publication before his death. [19]

Usually the posthumous work was justified by the efficacy of its content in furthering the work of the church. John Beale typically declares that to leave the work of Samuel Hieron unpublished would be "but to bury a talent in the earth." [20] But often enough the writer himself seems the primary consideration. Doubtless the apologists would have argued against this distinction; the writer was valued because of his works. Yet the emphasis on the man himself, almost as a personality, in the

---

[19]Sibbes, *Works*, III, 5.
[20]Hieron, *Works*, ep. ded. to *The Sermons*.

prefaces tended to elevate some writers into classics, into important literary figures, and to sanction within the framework of puritanism a genuinely literary fame. For instance, Henry Holland writes that Richard Greenham's "name, being so precious," has given the deceased minister "a second life on earth." [21] The writer of a preface to a work by Sibbes exhorts his readers to "behold, first, the man, secondly, the matter." [22] One can almost see developing a tradition of literary fame comparable to the secular. The main difference seems to be that whenever the comment is extended, the immortality ascribed to the author becomes dependent on the religious value of his work, with his personality and style only subsidiary considerations. The immortality sought by Shakespeare and Ovid was to be derived primarily from artistic achievement and was often expected to include the total personality, with its loves, hates, and ambitions. Insofar as the puritans valued the man himself, they thought of him chiefly as an example. Since example was one method of preaching, the revival or preservation of an exemplary man depended in large part on the utility of his sermons. Among the puritans, then, literary immortality was achieved in the same way as reputation for excellent preaching.

Some such theory explains Ferdinand Archer's commendatory lines prefixed to Samuel Bolton's *Dead Saint*:

> But is there left no transcript here beneath,
> Of that fair copy, rent from us by death?
> Yes. Turn these pages (Reader) —thou wilt see,
> His every line breathes immortality. [23]

The language of printing makes the point aptly. The dead saint, whose life and works were exemplary, was a copy of the saving word. His written words are a transcript of his life; in them he preaches by life and writing both. His fame, though immortal, is not the worldly applause gained by the secular poets,

---

[21]*The Workes of . . . M. Richard Greenham* (1605), 273.

[22]Sibbes, *Works*, VI, 537; preface to *The Bride's Longing*, by G. H. (identified by Grosart as George Hughes).

[23]Samuel Bolton, *The Dead Saint Speaking to Saints and Sinners Living* (1657), prefatory verses.

but the "fame in heaven" of Milton's *Lycidas,* if we interpret
Archer's verses in the light of an interesting tradition reported
by Edmund Calamy: "It is the opinion of some learned men,
that the saints who are now triumphing in Heaven, have an
augmentation of glory bestowed upon them, according to the
good they do after their deaths by sermons preached, or books
written, while they were living. Instance is given in the Apostle
Paul, whose glory in Heaven, say they, is increased according
as men are converted by reading of his epistles." [24] Calamy offers
the tradition as an inducement to the publication of the works
of dead ministers by their friends. However it served that purpose, it must have been, for all who accepted it, a powerful inducement to publish their religious works.

But all publications, posthumous or otherwise, met an objection from which vocal preaching was free. No puritan complained that there was, or suggested that there could be, too
much preaching, while complaints, both argumentative and
apologetic, against the number of books were frequent. Among
the earlier puritans, Hieron complained of "the scribbling age"
in which men had "even made the times to surfeit with their
needless papers." [25] After the triumph of puritanism, John Collinges decried the "writing age" and called for less writing and
more practicing, [26] while Edward Reynolds was disturbed by
"the groaning of the press." [27] But many of the objectors wrote
prolifically. Perhaps they were less impressed by the paradox of
complaining about the number of books while they increased
it because of the deeper paradox, underlying all of their literary
activity, that many books seemed to be necessary while the
Bible was all-sufficient. Precedents were occasionally cited in an
author's expression of uneasiness; George Hutcheson typically
appropriated the words of Luther, "who professed, if he thought
his writings would take up men's time from reading the Scriptures, he would, like Saturn, devour his own children." [28]

---

[24] Taylor, *Works,* I, ep. ded.
[25] Hieron, *Works,* ep. ded. to *The Back-Parts of Jehovah.*
[26] John Collinges, *A Cordial for a Fainting Soul* (1652), sig. A3v.
[27] Reynolds, *Works,* II, iv.
[28] George Hutcheson, *A Brief Exposition on the XII Small Prophets* (1657),
sig. A4v.

Very often, however, the puritans made exceptions, discounting objections to books, in theory as well as in practice, even while they stated the objections. In an extended defense of the proliferation of books, Thomas Manton justifies all the writing the press can turn out. Granting that "there is no end of books," that "all complain there is enough written," that "useless pamphlets are grown almost as great a mischief as the erroneous and profane," and that "it were well if in this scribbling age there were some restraint," Manton develops an extensive argument for more writing. He argues, conventionally enough, that the devil and his stratagems must be countered with good books and that the changing circumstances of the church require new guides to application of fundamental, unchanging principles. Then his argument, though no less platitudinous, becomes much more significant for literature in general, for he adduces stylistic considerations as further justification of writing. Basing his argument on the unimpeachable example of the Bible, he calls attention to the variety of style and tone in both Testaments, the contrasts between the "lofty, courtly style of Isaiah" and the "priestly, grave style of Jeremiah," and between the "sublime and seraphical" tone of John and the "rational and argumentative" tone of Paul. An example of diversity of style more modern and also of great authority he finds in the puritan utopia, Geneva, where Farel "thundered," Viret "piped . . . sweetly," and Calvin "taught . . . learnedly and solidly." Variety of style was thus sanctioned by the Holy Spirit and proved by its results in Geneva. [29]

Manton's argument deserves special attention only because he gave examples. The same reasoning lies behind the more aggressive defense made by John Hart, who paraphrases an unnamed "Right Reverend Father of the Church" to the effect that "if a thousand several men had all written on these several subjects, yet he could wish them all printed," because of differences in style and method of presentation. [30] The idea was expressed in an image that became commonplace; in Hieron's

---

[29]Sibbes, *Works*, III, 3-4.
[30]John Smith, *Essex Dove* (1637), sig. A3v.

words, "All stomachs we see are not alike: One kind of dressing pleaseth one, which hath no relish with another, and yet the same meat ordered after another fashion, may fit his appetite also." [31] The principle could be used to justify simple repetition, the publishing of a work that contained no new material, and Thomas Gataker did argue, "I know it will not be distasteful to hear or read a good point more than once or twice inculcated." [32] Finally, some could maintain that various "orthodox" books were not so many separate books because all knowledge is but one book, just as "all the prophets and apostles make but one Bible." [33]

Had the ministers accepted without reservations the value of writing, statements of the religious aims of their writing would have been superfluous. Yet, in a surprising number of works the author protests, argues, or specifies the religious purpose of his work. Whether he treats a new subject or follows a well-worn path, the puritan writer frequently makes explicit his religious purpose, the highest form of which is to preach the word by writing. The aim of preaching is generally taken for granted. The surprisingly large number of statements of pur-pose, made usually in general, commonplace terms, in itself suggests an uneasiness about writing.

Jeremiah Dyke's dedicatory epistle to Daniel Dyke's *Two Treatises* is so phrased that it might serve as a composite preface for most puritan works. Dyke grants that "but one book is necessary," the Bible, and, in keeping with tradition, cites Luther, whose "love to this Book, and the reading of it, made him hate his own books, and wish them lost." But Luther's works "yet were of . . . excellent use," and so is the book Dyke is publishing. By his action he intends, as Daniel Dyke had in his preaching, "to further the common good of all good Christians, in awakening and stirring them up to the conscionable discharge of teaching and right ordering their families, to the honour of God,

---

[31]Hieron, *Works*, preface to *The Preacher's Plea*.

[32]Gataker, *Certain Sermons*, 236.

[33]Sibbes, *Works*, IV, 310 (preface to *Exposition of II Corinthians iv*, signed by Ashe, Nalton, and Church).

their own, and the good of many souls." [34] The statement would
have been accepted by the writer of almost any preface, though
most commonly a similar idea was condensed into the adjectives
"serviceable" or "useful," with the religious context implied. Occasionally the didactic aim was more specific, as in Henry Smith's
Examination of Usury, where the preface contains the order,
"Go my book, like David against Goliah, and fight the Lord's
battles against usurers." [35]

Often, even when a work was patently didactic and all other
objections to publication had been removed, the author felt
constrained to reconcile the fact of publication with the humility
proper to a minister. Accusations of vanity were frequently an-
ticipated. A preface to Hieron's works contains a simple assertion: "He was not so vainglorious, as to publish books for his
own glory." [36] But more often, the writer or printer was careful
to state a specific reason cogent enough to bypass the issue of
vanity. Significant is the monotonous regularity with which the
ministers who preached before Parliament by invitation cited a
government order as a reason, often the sole reason, for publication. William Goode is typical in his modesty: "I could have
drawn many strong arguments from mine own weakness against
the publishing of this sermon, had not your desire deprived me
of my freedom." [37]

Many who were not forced by the authorities to obtrude their
unpolished works on the public were compelled to yield to the
solicitations of friends. Gataker reveals some vanity while trying
to deny it. "Conscious of the rawness" of his funeral sermon on
Richard Stock, he was "the more backward at first to yield to
the importunity of those (not a few) who both by letters and
words of mouth were very instant and urgent for the publishing
of it." [38] Arthur Hildersam is slightly more modest and more
typical when he declares that his reluctance to publish his "un-
worthy" lectures was overcome, after he had demurred for many

[34]Daniel Dyke, *Two Treatises* (1616), sigs. A2v-A3.
[35]Henry Smith, *Sermons* (1675), 75.
[36]Hieron, *Works*, "To the Reader," pt. II, by R. Hill.
[37]William Goode, *The Discoverie of a Publique Spirit* (1645), sig. A2v.
[38]Gataker, *Certain Sermons*, 254.

years: "I am now at length (through the importunity of sundry that think better of them than myself would ever do) enforced to give way that they may be published." [39]

A reason for publishing that the puritans had in common with the dramatists they condemned was piracy. Like any literary work for which a demand existed, a sermon might be written down in shorthand or from memory, or an injudicious friend might borrow a private copy and turn it over to the booksellers—if we are to believe the prefaces. A corrected edition was then necessary to save the minister's reputation for orthodoxy. Often enough, however, the writer expressed concern not only over doctrinal errors and imperfections that might distort the meaning of his work, but for his literary reputation as well. William Perkins warns the reader in an "Advertisement" that a work circulating under the title *Perkins upon the Lord's Prayer* is "faulty both in the matter and manner of writing"; specifically, some pages "are so penned the reader cannot know what was my meaning." Therefore he considers it his duty to publish an accurate text, even though the exposition of the subject "is already sufficiently performed of others." [40] Simeon Ashe declares that he has published a work to correct the errors made when it was written down in shorthand while he preached. [41] Edward Reynolds cites a predicament of St. Jerome to show that his own problem has a venerable antecedent; in both instances a copy of a work written for private use was given to a friend who insisted on publishing it. Reynolds has accepted the publication as a *fait accompli* and has agreed to revise the work. [42] William Bridge finds that his experience with the errors in the printing of one of his works allies him with Martial, whose protest to the printer he quotes and translates:

[39] Arthur Hildersam, *CVIII Lectures upon the Fourth of John* (1647), sig. A2.

[40] *The Works of . . . W. Perkins* (1603), "Advertisement" to *An Exposition of the Lord's Prayer.*

[41] Simeon Ashe, *A Support for the sinking Heart in times of distresse* (1642), sig. A2v.

[42] Reynolds, *Works*, III, iii.

> O Fidentine, a book of mine
> Thou printedst with my will;
> And yet not mine, but it is thine,
> Because it's printed ill.

Thus Bridge justifies a second edition. [43]

Occasionally, and with some egotism, the preacher cited other compulsions, such as the appropriateness of the time or the exigencies of controversy, which required him to write in order to supply needed advice or to defend some cause. Francis Woodcock thought the subject of one of his sermons "a text so every way apposite and concerning," that "it should not want a means whereby it might be sometimes remembered." [44] Samuel Bolton, convinced that his sermon was most appropriate to the state of the kingdom at the time, found reasons in Ecclesiastes for publishing it: "The wisest man tells us that to every thing there is a season, and experience tells us the present timing of things to that particular season is one of the highest acts of practical wisdom." [45] In these and many similar instances, the compulsion appears subjective enough to make the author suspect of rationalization. But such arguments are only a step removed from a perfectly logical justification of writing, the need to refute errors, which was urged often enough amid the numerous controversies of the day. William Twisse pleads typically that he would not have written on the Sabbatarian controversy had someone else come forth to refute the arguments of John Prideaux, which were gaining wide acceptance. [46] In the same battle, Robert Cleaver argues that he and his allies are "not mere voluntaries in this controversy, but necessarily urged thereto, as pressed soldiers; we begin not the quarrel, but only justify the truth of our doctrine and cause as defendants." [47]

The pervasive didacticism in these statements of the function of writing does not separate them entirely from traditional lit-

---

[43]Bridge, *Works*, V, 198.

[44]Francis Woodcock, *Lex Talionis* (1646), ep. ded.

[45]Samuel Bolton, *Deliverance in the Birth* (1647), sig. A2v.

[46]William Twisse, *Of the Morality of the Fourth Commandement* (1641), sig. C4.

[47]Robert Cleaver, *A Declaration of the Christian Sabbath* (1625), ep. ded.

erary theory. Superficially, the puritan statements seem to have
no connection with the literary theory of the poets, but many
of the differences can be explained· as adaptations of secular
theory to religious works. Secular writers also insisted that literature had a didactic, or at least formative, aim; in their version
of Horace's dictum, the aim was to profit by pleasing. Puritan
ministers used the terms profit and pleasure often enough, but
with qualifications or changes of emphasis. Samuel Bolton adopts
a puritan logic when he says that his work "will profit, and
therefore should please," [48] a statement that Horace and Sidney
would have approved in part, but not wholly. Edward Leigh
seems perfectly traditional in calling Whately's *Prototypes* "both
pleasant and profitable," but the pleasure lies in "the explaining
of divers stories" and in their "application," not in the aesthetic
appeal of the stories themselves or in the entertainment they
provide. [49] John Geree and William Greenhill move yet farther
from the secular meaning of the phrase when they inform the
"Christian Reader" that if he is "knowing" and "experienced
in the ways of Christ," he may find both delight and profit in
Thomas Shepard's *The First Principles*. [50] And the four ministers
who signed the preface to Pyncheon's *On the Sabbath* limit the
"great profit and delight" to "the serious reader." [51] The qualifications, together with the subjects of the treatises, indicate that
the puritans were turning phrases from secular theory to their
own distinct use. Yet the act of borrowing is a sort of tribute, and
the fact that the terms are used at all indicates that the puritans
saw their writings as part of the total corpus of literature, not
as something unique or so far unlike other literature that the
same critical standards could not be applied to them.

Other echoes of Renaissance literary theory are also to be
found. The puritans, as we have seen, justified posthumous publications largely by the argument that the dead preacher was
an example of virtuous living. Logically, therefore, Gataker

---

[48] Samuel Bolton, *The Sinfulnes of Sin* (1646), 2.

[49] Whately, *Prototypes*, preface.

[50] Thomas Shepard, *The First Principles of the Oracles of God* (1655), preface.

[51] William Pyncheon, *The Sabbath* (1654), sig. A2. The signers are Thomas
Clendon, Elidad Blackwell, John Sheffield, and Thomas Stevens.

quotes Aristotle, "Good examples . . . are of great force," in a funeral sermon upon a minister, to justify talking about the man himself. The conservative view was that the funeral sermon should be sparing of encomiums, but Gataker apparently believes that he is duly considerate of the welfare of his hearers in the "propagating and perpetuating of the memory of so worthy a servant of God." [52] Henry Burton finds it possible to justify an autobiography on the same grounds; citing the examples of Moses, David, and Paul, he argues that he has the ability at first hand "to give a just account to God's people of that divine support and comfort which it pleased the Lord to uphold me with, in all my trials." [53] Where Sidney commended the imaginative example as superior to reality, the puritans tried to find an approximation of the ideal within actuality itself; and, in a way, biography became their equivalent of epic or drama.

Biography and autobiography could be and usually were as explicitly didactic as any sermon. But their commemoration of the individual was akin to the use of a literary work as a memorial. Inevitably one finds echoes of the classical theme embodied by Shakespeare in "not marble nor the gilded monuments." Gataker presents a funeral sermon as "a private monument" and a "memorial" to the deceased. [54] Thomas Beard recalls Horace and Ovid in his hope that "I, being old, and ready to lay down this earthly tabernacle, might leave some lively monument behind me." [55] The modern reader may wonder at Beard's eagerness to be immortalized by *The Theatre*

---

[52] Gataker, *Certain Sermons*, 211. Probably the two best known puritan biographies are Baxter's *Breviate of the Life of Mrs. Margaret Baxter* and Lucy Hutchinson's *Memoirs of the Life of Colonel Hutchinson*. Although the strength of the personal feeling that caused them to be written and in large part accounts for their vitality makes them atypical, they are consistent with puritan statements of the function of biography.

[53] *A Narration of the Life of Mr. Henry Burton* (1643), sig. A2v. In Bunyan's *Grace Abounding*, the title itself justifies the autobiography. On the function of biographies and autobiographies as case histories in the struggle for salvation and as examples of the workings of Providence, see Murdock, "The 'Personal Literature' of the Puritans," Chapter 4 of *Literature and Theology*.

[54] Gataker, *Saint Stevens Last Will and Testament* (1638), sig. A2.

[55] Thomas Beard, *The Theatre of God's Iudgments* (1631), sig. A3.

of God's Judgements, an encyclopaedia of catastrophes sent as punishments for sin by a God who reveled in poetic justice. But Beard, concerned with the efficacy of fear as an aid to regeneration, doubtless saw himself in the tradition of the Old Testament prophets, and was unaware that his naive hope would, through his probably unconscious use of a secular commonplace, invite comparison with the vanity of poets.

The spectrum of reasons for publishing thus ranges from the most strictly religious to those with secular overtones. The cumulative impression is that the puritans felt the creative impulse and channeled it, sometimes with effort, into their literature of religious and moral edification. Inevitably they remind one of Milton, writing controversial pamphlets and channeling his long-unfulfilled aim to write a patriotic epic into his epic defenses of the English people.

Often the prefatory statements testify to the existence of less eloquent Miltons. One inevitably thinks of *Areopagitica* when he reads John Goodwin's tribute to books. The book is hard to distinguish from its author, he writes, "the book being but the mind of a man, and the mind of a man being the man himself." [56] Nor is Milton alone, or even merely one of a few, in his belief in freedom of the press. Too often we think of Thomas Edwards as the typical puritan in his attitude toward the publication of opinions differing from his own; we forget the numerous writers whom he flayed in *Gangraena,* who would never have agreed on censorship in practice. Nearly all puritans thought that the press was disseminating error, but for many, perhaps most, the remedy was to write and publish the truth as they saw it. Implicit in their very refusal to ask for stricter censorship and their eagerness to combat error is the profoundly humanistic assumption that the truth will emerge from controversy. Occasionally the statements become as explicit, though not so eloquent, as Milton's. *Areopagitica* is recalled again in a preface signed by Ashe, Nalton, and Church. Affirming that "good books are the baskets that preserve excellent lessons," the writers "bless God for the writings of his servants." They acknowledge that the

---

[56]Sibbes, *Works,* V, 4 (preface to *The Christian Work*).

press "may multiply errors," and that a "multitude not only of vain but blasphemous treatises" has been published and has done harm. But their conclusion is similar to Milton's: "The press is as open to the truth as error, and truth has been as nimble-heeled as error. God never yet suffered any Goliath to defy him, but he raised up a David to encounter him." [57]

By filling the bookshops and passing on to future libraries an abundance of edifying works, the puritans did not belie their esteem for the Bible and for preaching. They were firm believers in the ability of the printed word to achieve its aims, in its capacity to effect good or evil. Sometimes its very importance led them to advocate and practice censorship, but for many the answer was to be found in more writing by the orthodox or right-minded. The press was to be made a valuable instrument in the establishing of the rule of the saints, in the work of rescuing souls from damnation. The didactic aim was supreme, and they differed as a group from other writers in a greater emphasis on the profitable and less concern for the "pleasant," or aesthetic, aspects of a work. But the difference was not great enough to keep them from often considering themselves literary men of their day. Like any writers, they had their literary tradition with its classics: Hieron, Greenham, Smith, Perkins, Sibbes, to name only a few. Like their secular counterparts they worried about their literary reputations; and common circumstances of publication, including the frequent recourse to piracy of texts, gave similar excuses for the vanity of authorship to the dramatist with his stage-play and to his arch-foe, the puritan minister, with his sermon against the stage.

[57] *Ibid.*, IV, 309 (preface to *Exposition of II Corinthians iv*) .

CHAPTER 3

Brevity, Perspicuity, Spirituality

LOOKING UPON THEMSELVES not only as preachers but also as writers, as literary men working in a specialized area of writing, the puritans inevitably developed theories of organization and style within their field. Most of the theories have only indirect significance for other forms of literature; for instance, the structure of a puritan sermon could be duplicated in a commentary on the Bible, but hardly elsewhere. The theory of style could and did have a more general significance that has been universally recognized, and today the puritans share the blame and praise with the Royal Society for having ended the baroque period in English prose and brought about the development of modern prose style. Puritan "plain style," as it is universally called, was a successful competitor with the richness and complexity of Donne and Browne and a precursor of the relative austerity, but increased lucidity, of Dryden and his contemporaries.

No aspect of puritan literary theory and practice has been so often discussed as the plain style; every study of puritanism gives it some attention. Inevitably, when one approaches it he must travel over some ground that has been carefully surveyed and mapped by others. But some unexplored areas still remain; to abandon the metaphor, some significant questions have not been answered fully. For one thing, we are not certain to what extent the puritans deliberately thought of their stylistic theory as applicable to literature in general. The question may appear superfluous, since at least some effect on all forms of English prose can be taken for granted, but whether an effect has been produced deliberately or unwittingly is a question with significant implications for knowledge of the forces that shape literary developments.

Moreover, although we now know that puritan plain style was a highly artful style, not a rejection of literary effects, the suggestion remains that its roots were in asceticism, that it was essentially negative in its avoidance of literary sophistication even though it was directed toward the positive end of greater effectiveness in preaching and writing. We should still ask if the theory behind it was a theory of a new simple style, or a theory of a simplification of old style. By advocating plain style were the puritans thinking only of removing complexities from a highly developed art to achieve their particular aims more effectively, or were they trying to substitute one kind of art for another? And, however we answer that question, we should know also if the puritans thought the old art bad per se, or merely useless in their special circumstances.

Finally, we know that puritan belief in the plain style was not entirely uniform and inflexible, that there were differences in both theory and practice. We may ask, then, how wide and how significant the differences were and what caused them.

The style of the puritan sermon is in itself a large and recently well-cultivated subject. One can summarize relevant current studies by starting with Haller's demonstrations of the rich imagery, careful organization, and generally deliberate artistry employed by the puritans. Resulting conclusions must be qualified slightly by Fisch's reservation that surviving printed sermon material is the work of the "more literary-minded" puritans, though this reservation applies also to Anglican sermons and is therefore unimportant in any comparative study or outline of differences in puritan and Anglican style. More significant to an understanding of the puritan theory of style is Haller's observation that the puritans made use of traditional pulpit techniques which survived from the Middle Ages through the Reformation and its controversies. [1] In sermon style the Anglican minister was more the innovator, and the puritans often

---

[1] See Haller, *Rise of Puritanism*, 133, 140-41; Harold Fisch, "The Puritans and the Reform of Prose Style," *English Literary History*, XIX (1952), 233.

rejected Anglican styles less because of a radical desire for more thorough reformation than because of a conservative suspicion of stylistic innovations and fads. John Collinges, for instance, contrasts the old-fashioned "plain English" of the godly preacher with the new "Seneca-sermons," thinking, perhaps, of Donne himself, and declares that "wit is the soul's worst carver." [2]

In the sermons, which form a large and perhaps the most deliberately artistic part of the puritan literary output, a carving of the soul was the chief aim. The preacher sought to arouse his audience to a consciousness of human sinfulness and God's mercy, and to move it to take action; hence the stress on the "liveliness," or vividness, of the spoken word. Whatever his theory of style might exclude, concreteness and the imagery of everyday life, with their immediacy and strength of effect, had to be part of his repertory. A completely bare, dull, bland style was simply beside the point. This the puritans seldom bothered to explain, and we can also take for granted that the term "plain style" comprehended a measure of vividness and color, not merely as seasoning, but as an integral, basic ingredient.

In polemic and expository treatises, clarity, logical consistency, and general intelligibility to the thoughtful, though not necessarily learned, reader were the primary and relatively simple requirements. Basically, the plain style was advocated by the puritans for vocal preaching. But the written sermon and treatise were also a kind of preaching, as we have seen, and the same kind, if not the same degree, of plainness was logically proper to written sermons and to all other works designed to explain and apply the word of Scripture. Characteristically, the puritans turned to the Bible for directions concerning style and found them in I Corinthians 2:4: "And my speech and my preaching was not with enticing words of man's wisdom, but in demonstration of the spirit and of power." The relatively ambiguous words were interpreted by William Perkins, the most influential puritan theological writer of his time, as a directive to "observe an admirable plainness and an admirable powerfulness." [3]

---

[2] Collinges, *The Spouse under the Apple-Tree* (1649), ep. ded.
[3] Perkins, *Of the Calling of the Ministerie* (1618), 430. Other Biblical texts were cited, but this one seems to occur most frequently. Perkins is

The term *powerfulness,* ubiquitous in puritan comments on preaching, is less difficult than it seems. Here it can be dismissed with the observation that it refers more to the method of delivery and the psychological effect of the sermon than to the verbal content or stylistic technique. It names, in fact, the universally desired effect upon the emotions of the hearers. Plainness, on the other hand, designates style and diction and has a surprising variety of interpretations. In various contexts the puritans offered supplementary adjectives as glosses.

In a life of Whately, by Henry Scudder, the words of St. Paul are applied verbatim to Whately and supplemented by the explanation that his preaching was "plain" and that "he was much against all such preaching as was light, vain, scenical, impertinent, raw, and undigested." [4] Plainness apparently lies somewhere between rawness and frivolity, but the terms are not antithetical; at best we derive the general impression that Whately's sermons were carefully composed, but not too highly ornamented. The various adjectives do add up at least to an impression, even while they testify to the difficulty the puritans had in defining the Biblical terms. Other attempts at explanation help define by exclusion. Reynolds, in his *Preaching of Christ,* explains "with enticing words of man's wisdom" as "with ostentation of wit or human elocution, with rhetorical sophisms, or plausible insinuating deceptions, as Cicero somewhere boasteth that he hath dazzled the eyes of his followers." [5]

Though Reynolds disparages Cicero, he does not condemn pagan literature and literary techniques, as he shows elsewhere. Few puritans advocated aesthetic obscurantism. Even Samuel How, the preaching cobbler, who was extreme in his rejection of human learning as an aid to the understanding or interpreting of Scripture, writes with some uneasiness of his style, and that in a mere argumentative treatise. Admitting the "rudeness"

---

quoted in nearly all discussions of plain style. For thorough discussions of the origin, purpose, function, and use of the plain style, see especially Haller, *Rise of Puritanism,* 129-34, and Miller, *New England Mind,* 331-62.

[4] Whately, *Prototypes,* sig. A3.

[5] Reynolds, *Works,* V, 347.

of his work, he argues that "if any shall except against the matter, for the rudeness of it, as that it is without form or learning, all such are to know that it is but suitable to the whole argument, and that if it should be otherwise, I should condemn that in practice, which I justify in words, and so make myself a trespasser." [6] The apologetic note is clearly discernible, and it is to be found in countless other prefaces. James Nalton's remark that his sermon before Parliament is a "plain, homely piece" is part of an apology for lack of literary talent. [7] Even when the preacher tries to justify his rudeness, his arguments show an awareness that he is going against a literary tradition, for he does not deny his work an impact on the reader or suggest that it may fail in its effect. The puritans respected the values of conventional literary style deeply enough to feel a need to explain its absence even in sermons and doctrinal treatises that might, conceivably, achieve their effects without it.

One of the most common types of apologetic explanations of plain style is illustrated by a dedicatory epistle of Hieron, who explains that he is "living here by God's providence, in a country congregation," and for that reason has tried not to "exceed the conceit of common hearers." [8] Elsewhere he refers to his "plain and country-course style of handling" his subject. In this context, with its stress on the rusticity of the congregation, Hieron's espousal of "such plainness as might best affect the conscience" and "a purposed avoiding of that over-abundant artificialness" which is "much in workmanship, but in profit nothing" is not absolute, but relative, depending upon a specific auditory and a specific aim. In fact, Hieron says explicitly that the same "way of handling" a subject is not suited to all hearers, and he accepts literary craftsmanship as a relevant value when he describes his style as a sort of *via media* between the "over-homely" which, he says, "were ill-befitting the oracles of God" and that which would "exceed, either by affectations of words,

---

[6]Samuel How, *The Sufficiencie of the Spirits Teaching Without Humane Learning* (1644), sig. A4v.

[7]James Nalton, *Delay of Reformation Provoking Gods Further Indignation* (1646), sig. A3v.

[8]Hieron, *Works*, ep. ded. to *The Spiritual Sonne-ship*.

or by a too exact couching or carriage of the particulars to be treated on . . . the reach of the meanest and least-gifted hearer." [9]

The welfare of the "least gifted hearer" appears again and again as the justification of the plain style. Late in puritan history John Owen says of James Durham's *Practical Exposition of the Ten Commandments* that the work "is accommodated unto the meanest capacities, which is the greatest excellency of discourses of this nature." The accommodation requires exclusion of "all ornaments of speech, everything that diverts from plainness, sobriety, and gravity." [10] Apparently many of the puritans felt that style had a lowest common denominator of plainness, that a sermon or treatise could be written so that it would be meaningful to all possible readers and hearers. Yet would this style be effective with the more learned? Some did not bother with that problem. Samuel Clarke reports that John Dod "took great care to speak to the meanest capacity . . . saying he must stoop to the lowest capacity, and if he could reach them, all others might help themselves.' [11] The theory is fiercely democratic, but of all the noted puritan preachers Dod was the least concerned with publication and literary fame, and the most ready to ignore the more sophisticated members of his congregation.

Most puritan writers were less inclined to tell their readers to help themselves and more willing to argue that their work contained something of value and interest to educated readers as well as to the masses. Arthur Dent writes, typically but with more naiveté of expression than most, that "here is no great matter in learning, wit, art, eloquence, or ingenious invention (for I have herein specially respected the ignorant and vulgar sort, whose edification I chiefly aim at) yet somewhat there is, which may concern the learned, and give them some contentment." [12] One way to reach all readers is, of course, to mix two levels of subject or style, as Dent implies he has done. But an approach

---

[9] *Ibid.*, ep. ded. to *Penance for Sinne.*

[10] James Durham, *A Practical Exposition of the X. Commandements* (1675), the third "Epistle to the Reader."

[11] Samuel Clarke, *A Martyrologie* (1652), 414.

[12] Dent, *Plain Man's Pathway*, sig. A2v.

suitable to all levels of understanding at one time would be much more desirable. Robert Cleaver states the problem accurately and affirms that a solution is possible, citing the authority of the Bible for the use of a plain style to cover the whole intellectual spectrum of readers. In his exposition of Proverbs 1:5-6, he raises the logical objection: "If your sayings and proverbs be so plain and easy that the simple may sound them, and the child may comprehend them, what good will they do the wise and learned?" Solomon's answer is given in images that can be traced back through Boccaccio to St. Gregory's *Moralia* on Job: "Yea (saith he) the greatest clerks, and deepest divines, may gather information from them, as well as the vulgar and meaner sort of people. They are shallow enough for a little child to wade, and deep enough for a great Leviathan to swim in." [13] The image only widens the dilemma, but Cleaver is not trying to prove, or even to explain; he merely states a premise from which the most uncompromising advocates of the plain style worked.

Others, of course, accepted a diversity of styles as logical and inevitable. Hieron, in the quotations given above, at least implied that a sermon addressed to a more learned congregation than his might be differently composed. Robert Bolton made the particular audience the criterion; admitting that he has combined into one work five sermons delivered upon separate occasions, he explains that all were addressed to "a most judicious and intelligent auditory; therefore there is a continuance of matter, coherence, and style." [14] If the explanation has any logical meaning, Bolton assumes that a preacher can be expected to master various styles and that plainness is not always appropriate. But if a man preached to the same congregation regularly, he might develop a personal idiom. To the literary executors of Sibbes, the preacher's individual style as well as

---

[13] Cleaver, *A Briefe Explanation of the Whole Booke of the Proverbs of Solomon* (1615), 4-5. W. P. Ker notes that the image was "a favorite quotation" with Boccaccio; see *The Dark Ages* (London: William Blackwood and Sons, 1904), 135.

[14] Robert Bolton, *A discourse about the state of True Happinesse* (1631), preface.

his spiritual tone was a trademark of authorship, proving the sermon was really his: "If any should doubt of these sermons as if they should not be truly his, whose name they bear, let him but observe the style, and the excellent and spiritual matter herein contained, and he will, we hope, be fully satisfied." [15] Gouge betrays some literary self-consciousness, some idea of an individual, personal style, even while he makes the audience all-important. His *Dignitie of Chivalry* is not in his characteristic style, he explains, because "I had respect to the kind of auditory before which I spoke. Among soldiers, I endeavor to speak soldier-like." [16]

But the audience was not the only criterion, and sometimes it was not the most important one. For many puritans, the subject determined the style, and plainness was recommended not only because of its didactic efficacy, but because of its suitability and propriety to the task of interpreting Scripture as well. We have noted that many puritans were uneasy about publishing books when the Bible alone was considered sufficient. Logically, many also felt that it was harmful, impious, or at least useless to vie with the Bible in excellence of style. One point of view is expressed by John Preston: "There is no art, science, tongue, knowledge, or eloquence in the world that hath such excellency in time as the Word hath." It follows for Preston that "he that useth eloquence in the preaching of the Word doth nothing else but draw the heart away from affecting the pure Word." [17] Closely related to this belief that the use of human eloquence is distracting and presumptuous is Gataker's assertion that all eloquence is vain when it is added to the words of God. He admits the plainness of his work, but insists it is suitable to his audience, not because the audience is necessarily unlearned, but because "the truth of God cannot but find good entertainment with all those that sincerely love and like it, although it come naked and bare, as best beseemeth it, or but meanly attired, not bedecked and set forth with such

[15] Sibbes, *Works*, II, 442 (ep. ded. to *The Glorious Feast of the Gospel*, signed by Arthur Jackson, James Nalton, and William Taylor).

[16] Gouge, *Works*, II, 406.

[17] John Preston, *Sinnes Overthrow* (1635), 102-103.

ornaments as the natural eye and ear only affect and regard." [18]
In other words, truth has a more effective, penetrating appeal
when the senses are not too thoroughly engaged by the mode of
presentation. This point of view is expressed even more clearly
by Gouge, who finds the plain style in the Bible itself; at least,
"all the fundamental points of Christian religion, necessary to
salvation, they are clearly and plainly set down." [19] Hieron avows
that Scripture has set the tone of his own style: "I have never
affected any other eloquence than that of the scripture." [20] Thus
the puritans developed a notion of decorum in style; to many
of them plainness meant appropriateness to the interpretation of
Scripture. By another path they came to the same conclusion as
Hieron: "In preaching I have ever counted plainness the best
eloquence." [21]

But during the age of puritanism, as today, the word "plain"
had ambivalent meanings: the laudatory signification of "clarity," and the pejorative signification of "rudeness." Many were
willing to accept the term in all meanings and connotations, to
embrace rudeness for the sake of the all-important clarity. But
a large number were so fastidious stylistically that they could
not praise a work for being plain, even apologetically. In an
effort to retain only the laudatory meanings, they brought into
use the words "perspicuous," and, less often, "perspicacious." At
the same time, as if to deny more explicitly the elaborateness
and prolixity accompanying rhetorical embellishment, they
adopted "brevity" as one of the highest terms of praise. The
goal was much like that of the Royal Society. Certainly Thomas
Sprat's ideal is foreshadowed by Richard Bernard's stated intention "to set down much matter in a few words, and to illustrate
the manifold precepts by evident examples briefly." [22] In Sprat's
own time it was paralleled by Clarke's fondness for the idea.
Clarke declared that his own aim was "to include much matter
in few words," and later he excused Hugh Broughton's cus-

[18]Gataker, *Certain Sermons*, 69-70.
[19]Gouge, *Works*, II, 162.
[20]Hieron, *The Abridgement of the Gospel* (1634), ep. ded.
[21]Hieron, *Works*, ep. ded. to *Truth's Purchase*.
[22]Richard Bernard, *The Faithfull Shepheard* (1607), sig. A4.

tomary harshness with the statement that Broughton's aim was "to speak much in few words." [23] The title pages of Hieron's *Doctrine of the Beginning of Christ* advertises his work as "short for memory, plain for capacity," to reassure the common reader. But Gouge has subtly changed the terms, and assures his readers that he has tried to be as "perspicuous and brief" as possible. [24] Then, in a preface to Sibbes's *A Heavenly Conference*, another term has been added, to give his style the highest praise that could be conveyed by the puritans in three words: he is said to have written with "brevity, spirituality, and perspicacity." [25]

The attitude reflected by this terminology is perhaps best explained by Henry Smith, who tried to clarify the difference between acceptable plainness and rudeness: "to preach simply is not to preach rudely, nor unlearnedly, nor confusedly, but to preach plainly and perspicuously." Smith objects to some of his contemporaries who "shroud and cover every rustical and unsavoury, and childish, and absurd sermon under the name of the simple kind of teaching," who preach too "barely, and loosely, and simply." [26] Smith here still uses "plain" as synonymous with "perspicuous," but he. rejects the connotations of crudeness or lack of sophistication. Many others, especially later in the puritan era, avoided the problem of defining "plain" by choosing partial synonyms.

The reaction against crudeness of style was strong enough to appear sometimes as an unequivocal advocacy of eloquence, an ostensible denial of the plain style. Among the older puritans, Greenham stressed the learning and eloquence of St. Paul as a model for Christian preachers, noting that the apostle was "read in Aratus, Epimenides, Menander, made Felix to tremble with his eloquence, was thought Mercury for his eloquence at Lycaonia, by the notable course and vein of all his epistles, not inferior to the writings of any of the heathen." Greenham seems to have chosen his examples to counter the usual interpretation

---

[23]Clarke, *The Lives of Sundry Eminent Persons in This Later Age* (1683), 2, 8.
[24]Gouge, *Works*, I, preface.
[25]Sibbes, *Works*, VI, 417 (signed by Ashe, Nalton, and Church).
[26]Henry Smith, *Sermons* (1675), 121.

of Paul's objection to the "enticing words of man's wisdom," to argue that the objection does not rule out stylistic graces. His prescription for the ministers is in the same spirit, as he quotes with approval an unnamed authority: "He observed that some speaking against eloquence, did savor much of a human spirit in their preaching, which is as evil or worse. For eloquence is not simply forbidden, but when it waiteth on carnal wisdom, for otherwise, joined with the power of the word and demonstration or evidence of the spirit, it is effectual; but human wisdom, very barren and destitute of eloquence, is evil."[27] Greenham does not explicitly reject the plain style; he points out that in itself it is no virtue. His argument may be simply an attempt, like Henry Smith's, to right the balance; but its whole force is exerted in defense of rhetorical and literary sophistication.

Even preachers who at times advocated the plain style as insistently as anyone would at other times praise eloquence in terms even more laudatory than Greenham's. Gataker, as we have seen, excused even rudeness because the word of God needed no ornaments. Yet in his funeral sermon on Richard Stock, in which he conventionally upheld the deceased as an example to the living, his ideal seems to be quite different. He says of Stock, "How well he was able not to express only, but to urge and press too, nor to confirm alone, but to commend also that that he delivered, with clear method, sound proofs, choice words, fit phrase, pregnant similitudes, plentiful illustrations, pithy persuasions, sweet insinuations, powerful enforcements, allegations of antiquity, and variety of good literature, that both the learnedst might receive satisfaction from him, and the very meanest and dullest also might reap benefit by him."[28] The social aim of the preacher, to reach the understanding of the common man, is reaffirmed by Gataker. But without telling how, he affirms also that the ideal was fulfilled by Stock through the use of a sophisticated and learned style. In other puritan obsequies, plainness of style was mentioned relatively seldom,

---

[27]Greenham, *Works*, 399-400.
[28]Gataker, *Abraham's Decease* (1627), 10. Most of this passage is quoted by Haller, *Rise of Puritanism*, 291.

while an eloquent or artful style was frequently adduced to the credit of the deceased. Nicholas Estwick, for another example, praises the "high strain of grave eloquence" attained by Robert Bolton. [29]

Sometimes, though rarely, a puritan writer drops a remark that implies clearly that a variety of styles may be needed for varied aims, within the didactic framework of all puritan writing. Dod and Cleaver are at times uncompromising in their loyalty to the plain style; yet in the preface to the *Brief Explanation of the Proverbs of Solomon*, they excuse their "homely kind of writing . . . devoid of all polishment and elegance," not for any of the reasons mentioned above, such as its intelligibility to the common reader, but because it is "but an exposition to inform the judgment in the meaning of the Scripture, and not a discourse to work upon the affections." [30] They imply that a rhetorical or persuasive aim might demand a polished style, or some elegance; for, as we have noted, the goal of preaching "powerfully" was to work upon the affections, to evoke in the hearer an emotional apprehension, as prerequisite to an intellectual, of his sinfulness and of the magnitude of God's mercy and the strictness of His justice. Consistently, then, a preacher who considered himself a mere transmitter of the word would have relatively less use for literary art, but one more conscious of his role as a moral leader and exhorter would need and use it all the more. The functions are difficult to separate, and perhaps the interlocking of their differences and similarities accounts for some of the differences in emphasis in puritan discussions of style.

The ambiguity is clearly illustrated by Reynolds, who wrote directly and systematically about literary graces of style. Because of the relative conservatism that led Reynolds to accept a bishopric after the Restoration, some historians may place him in a twilight zone of puritanism and account for any ambivalences in his attitude by positing a divided allegiance. Yet his participation in the Westminster Assembly and his secure tenure under

---

[29]Nicholas Estwick, *A Learned and Godly Sermon Preached . . . at the Funerall of Mr. Robert Bolton* (1633) , 66.

[30]Cleaver, *Brief Explanation of the Proverbs of Solomon*, preface.

the Commonwealth rank him clearly enough among the puritans. And his comments on style bear no individual or personal trademark; he differs from Greenham and Gataker only in being more explicit, and from many other puritans only in having commented more extensively on similar subjects. Almost every one of his statements could be found paraphrased somewhere among the writings of earlier or contemporary puritans. Nor can his ostensible inconsistencies be attributed to a development of his ideas; for comments identical in tenor appear both before and after statements that partially contradict them. Apparently, Reynolds' theory of style, like his religious beliefs, remained consistent, but was expressed in various ways as circumstances dictated.

In a dedicatory epistle to the House of Commons, Reynolds typically excuses his "plainness" on both the usual grounds: it is best suited "to the conscience of a penitent," and it is decorous and proper to the subject, for "the truth of God is indeed fuller of majesty when it is naked, then when adorned with dress of any human contribution." [31] The statement might have been made by How, though How would have spoken less confidently. But in an early philosophical treatise, published late in life as if to demonstrate that his opinions had not changed materially, Reynolds approves a wide range of styles. By implication, at least, he approves imitation of pagan classics, for he openly discounts the usual interpretation of St. Jerome's palinode. Obscurantists were fond of quoting Jerome on the dream in which an angel had beaten him for having been a Ciceronian rather than a Christian, for having been too fond of secular learning. But Reynolds calls the underlying idea a "melancholy fancy" and points out that elsewhere Jerome praised secular learning and admitted "that conceited vision of his to have been but a dream." Many puritans were ready to accept pagan works as objects of study in preparation for the ministry, though not as stylistic models for sermons; however, Reynolds' belief that the "spoils of Egypt" should be used to bedeck the

---

[31]Reynolds, *Works*, III, ep. ded. to *Seven Sermons on the Fourteenth Chapter of Hosea.*

temple of God implies that the spoils of Cicero's orations and rhetorical theories could be admitted even in the puritan pulpit. [32]

Reynolds writes more directly about style in his comment on the faculty of speech, which, in keeping with tradition, he calls the "gate of the soul" and the faculty whereby "man excelleth all other inferior creatures." Oratory is his main subject, but since Reynolds and his contemporaries often implied both spoken and written discourse by this term, unless they were writing specifically of the voice or gestures of a public speaker, the same principles of style and organization were applied to both speech and writing. Style is discussed by Reynolds under the headings of rhetorical "virtues" and rhetorical "vices." The virtues he emphasizes are "choice, purity, brevity, perspicuity, moderate acrimony and vehemency." The familiar shortness and plainness appear in their more Latinate dress with no suggestion that crudeness is admissible; and the remainder of the list presupposes a high degree of artistry. But the vices are even more useful in defining the proper style; they include "sordidness, tediousness, obscurity, flatness of conceit, arguteness and 'minutiae,' gaudiness, wordiness, and empty ostentation." Most of them represent specific departures from brevity and perspicuity, but in "sordidness" Reynolds condemns a vice that could accompany plainness, and in "ostentation" he looks beyond the quality and effect of the work into the motives of the speaker. [33]

Like many others, Reynolds believes that no one style is ideal for all occasions. But he does not emphasize use of the audience as the conditioning factor, perhaps because he takes its importance for granted. In his stated principle of decorum, the condition of the speaker is important: "It is not wisdom for a man in misery to speak with a high style, or a man in dignity with a creeping." This principle, reacting upon the puritan consciousness of man's wretched estate, would give further support to the use of plainness and the avoidance of literary graces. But the rhetorical form, determined by place, subject, and aim, is also

---

[32]*Ibid.,* VI, 6-7.
[33]*Ibid.,* 309-13.

an important consideration, for "the same speech may be excellent in an umbratile exercitation, which would be pedantical and smelling of the lamp, in a matter of serious and weighty debate." Reynolds' concept of decorum in style is generally consistent with Renaissance literary theory. [34]

His general discussion of style is consistent also with his specific directions for preaching, given in a sermon delivered after the Restoration, and it is in harmony with both his approval of Cicero and his praise of the plain style. The word is to be preached, he says, demonstratively, sincerely, wisely, boldly, meekly, affectionately, and "plainly, without unnecessary affectation or ostentation of the enticing words of man's wisdom, or of mere human and exotic wit and learning." The plain style would exclude the various rhetorical vices he had identified, but it does not preclude eloquence or artfulness. The literary imagination gets qualified approval, also, when Reynolds warns preachers that they should not "too much indulge nor loosen the reins unto luxuriancy of fancy in so solemn and serious a work as preaching the gospel, but proportion their ballast to their sail and temper their fancy with humility, piety, and prudence." [35] The treatment of fancy (or imagination) seems highly negative, but caution would be meaningless unless it were based on a solid conviction òf the worth of the faculty; Reynolds merely insists that it is not without faults. His caution suggests to the modern reader that many of the uncompromising approvals of the plain style may have been attempts to proportion the ballast to the sail in the sermons of younger ministers too prone to indulge literary inclinations.

In Reynolds' theory the word "plainness," qualified by adjectives that neutralize its pejorative meaning, is a term of praise. It has as its antithesis not ornamentation or elaboration, but ostentation. As the puritans rejected vaingloriousness as a motive for publication, so they condemned any display of artistic ability in style either for the sake of the art itself or for the sake of the writer's literary reputation. Yet they recognized

---

[34] *Ibid.*, 313.
[35] *Ibid.*, V, 400-403.

that an effective style had to be an artful one. To identify the kind of art that was needed, they borrowed from secular theory the anonymous dictum *ars est celare artem,* and interpreted it as a sanction of unobtrusive, unselfconscious artistry. Perkins, in the *Art of Prophesying,* gave the phrase the support of his great reputation: "The minister may, yea and must privately use at his liberties the arts, philosophy, and variety of reading, whilst he is framing his sermon; but he ought in public to conceal all these from the people and not to make the least ostentation. *Artis etiam est celare artem,* it is also a point of art to conceal art." [36] Whately had typically noted that "the arts of logic and rhetoric . . . prevail most when they are in such sort used, as they be least discerned" and that "it is believed as a great part of art to hide art." [37] Ironically, the phrase is used with equal insistence by Perkins and Whately, Jonson and Herrick; it was put to work in both puritan sermons and "Corinna's Going A-Maying." In time the phrase became synonymous with the virtues of perspicuity and brevity, and so familiar that it did not need to be quoted in full, or explained, except insofar as a new or unusual meaning was to be drawn from it. For instance, John Sedgwick comments on Sibbes that "his art was to hide his art, *est celare artem &c,* to say much in few words." [38] The hidden art is related to brevity here, in a way that is not explained, but the logic of the connection may be that since prolixity is naturally ostentatious, brevity, in contrast, requires a hidden art. In all its meanings, the phrase, used as a motto, directed the minister to preach and to write carefully and skilfully, to be plain only in the sense of being clear, not in the sense of being crude or truly simple. It enjoined him also to achieve simultaneously two almost antithetical aims: to use "few words" but "to say much."

The "matter" of the discourse was, of course, the pre-eminent concern. Yet we do not describe the puritan theory of style by saying that in it content was stressed to the neglect of form and

---

[36]Perkins, *The Arte of Prophecying* (1607), 133.
[37]Whately, *A Bride-Bush* (1623), 162.
[38]Sibbes, *Works,* V, 157.

manner. In fact, the basic content was already written in the Bible, and had the puritans ignored methods of presentation, they would logically have been content with reading, and no argument for the preaching ministry would have arisen. The common argument that many books on the same subject were good because dishes can be prepared in various ways for various tastes made style both incentive and excuse for writing.

Nor can we simply dismiss puritan style with the comment that a bare, unadorned style, eschewing literary devices, was the puritan norm. The statements quoted and paraphrased indicate that a "plain style" was a universal ideal, but that the term meant different things to different preachers and writers, and that only a few construed it to mean a style that ignored all literary techniques and avoided all rhetorical devices. If these few are considered atypical, the puritans appear to have held a complex theory of style which few ever explained logically. It was not a homogeneous or clearly defined theory, nor even a combination of theories. One can best describe it as a notion of the proper way to achieve the ideal of instructing and motivating the hearers and readers, a notion in which the ideal of clarity and the respect for the beauty and usefulness of literary arts were joined in an undefined and rather vague relation, neither in harmony nor discord, but in a taut bond which pulled the writer toward one or the other at various times. The apparently conflicting statements found among the writers and within the works of each of several individuals are best explained by differences in emphasis.

One of the two poles of puritan theory is illustrated vividly and in all its complexity by Hieron, the early advocate and practitioner of the plain style. He believes the preacher is "most eloquent, who in manner of speaking best entreth into every ordinary conceit," for "eloquence, not understood, benefits not." Yet, the preacher must try to reconcile disparate aims: "Our preaching must be learned, yet familiar; eloquent, and yet so plain, that it may truly be said of it, that if it be hid, it is hid to them that are lost." [39] The other pole is exemplified by the

---

[39]Hieron, *Works, The Preacher's Plea*, 534.

opinion of Joseph Caryl, whose preaching was frequently in demand by the Long Parliament. Caryl finds the Scriptures full of examples of the finest poetry, and its writers "over-matching all poets and heathen orators in depth of conceit, exactness of style, and flowers of rhetoric, as much as the sun doth a candle, or the spirits of wine the dregs of it." And Scripture is the example to be followed, for "it is our duty to make more than bare narratives and histories; we must cloth them with eloquence, and make oratory do homage to the service of God." But Caryl is not advocating every kind of clothing; his ideal is modified by a qualification: "Thus should we polish and garnish, embroider and bedeck the words of God, not with vain ostentation or pedantic pomp of words, but with sobriety and holy gravity." [40] Hieron and Caryl are not at odds; each is merely stressing one aspect of a complex ideal: to be eloquent, but not ostentatious; clear, but not rude.

[40]Joseph Caryl, *Englands Plus ultra* (1646), 29.

CHAPTER 4

Poems, Ballads, Romances

TODAY, WHEN the times of Shakespeare, Webster, and even Ford are looked upon as a golden age of English drama, the puritan attack on the Elizabethan and seventeenth-century stage is enough to brand the puritans as enemies of literature. Corroboration for this judgment can easily be found in the absence of literary work of first quality, with the stellar but inconclusive exception of Milton, in the writings of the puritans. The judgment can be supported by the decline of the seventeenth-century lyric during the religious and political hegemony of the puritans, and by the general antipathy of poets toward their puritan contemporaries. If this brand is merited, we should be able to find some puritan attacks on poetry and imaginative prose fiction, attacks similar in tone to the vehement denunciations of the stage. But while the puritans contributed numerous and redundant books, pamphlets, and lengthy incidental discussions to the stage controversy and expressed unanimous disapproval of the theatre, they were extremely reticent about nondramatic literature. That is, they wrote no books or pamphlets against it, or even about it. Their comments on it are generally brief, oblique, or inconclusive. This silence itself can be taken as evidence of asceticism, for it leaves their condemnation of one literary form unbalanced by extended praise of any other. But from prefaces and cursory mentions in sermons and treatises, one can reconstruct attitudes that more definitely explain the purport of their infrequent remarks and more validly establish the meaning of their silence.

In their discussions of the value of books, the puritans paid their respects to the value of the printed word and demonstrated a feeling that their kind of writing was of transcendent importance to the reading public. As practicing writers they developed . notion, however complex, of the proper style for their writings. In all their comments on these matters, they did not reject polite literature or deny it value, and they did not try deliberately to influence the formal aspects of any writing except their own—the sermon and the treatise. Nevertheless, they competed with poets and writers of prose tales for an audience, and they were aware of the competition.

Occasionally the competition was direct. Although the sermon and treatise now seem to be the characteristic form of puritan expression, the puritans by no means eschewed secular art forms, including poetry. [1] Primarily, as Perry Miller has explained, they regarded poetry "as a means to an end," and their vigorous, reiterated emphasis on matter, relegating form and style to an abjectly subordinate position, probably detracted from the artistic merit of their performances in verse. [2] Poetry, they believed, could, by working on the affections, help the preacher or catechizer deliver his message with greater impact; and the mnemonic advantages of rhythm and rhyme made verse more efficacious, didactically, than prose. But the puritan minister was doubtless untroubled by one part of Sidney's curse: he considered the utilization of a sonnet to win favor in love a highly improper use of a noble art, though, as we have seen, he did betray some concern for an epitaph, and wrote many elegies in verse. The practical, approved function of poetry in the puritan scheme of culture is well illustrated by Baxter: "Poetry," he wrote, "(as all inferior things) hath its conveniences and its inconveniences. The inconveniences are that matter is oft forced too much to stoop to words and syllables, and that conciseness keeps the matter from a full perception with any but well-prepared understandings. The conveniences are that it spareth

---

[1] See Murdock, *Literature and Theology*, for a study of puritan work in history, biography, autobiography, and poetry.

[2] Perry Miller and Thomas H. Johnson, *The Puritans* (New York: American Book Company, 1938), 547.

words, avoiding the redundancies and repetitions which oratory is usually guilty of, and teacheth exactness of expression. And that the delight of harmony (except in persons whose fantasy is herein impotent and maimed, as minds diseased by prejudice and melancholy) doth make the fantasy helpful to the mind, and as it expresseth affections, so doth it raise them." But this affective quality, Baxter promptly adds, is exploited by the devil in "lascivious, vain, and foolish poetry." [3]

This use of poetry by the devil frightened and antagonized many of the puritan writers. Significantly, and logically, their comments on popular secular writing are consistent—and correspondingly unanimous—with their denunciations of the stage. From before Perkins to the time of Baxter the puritans spoke almost as with one voice against the popular ballads and romances that provided idle reading for the less sophisticated members of their congregations. Perkins, in a brief discussion called "Of Writing," condemns "ballads, books of love, and idle discourses and histories" for "being nothing else but vain enticements and baits unto manifold sins." [4] Baxter, in *The Christian Directory*, condemns "playbooks, and romances, and idle tales"; [5] "the reading of vain books, playbooks, romances, and feigned histories"; [6] and, finally, "idle tales, and playbooks, and romances or love-books, and false bewitching stories." [7] The repetitions and variations in terminology help define the kinds of works that Baxter had in mind; in general, he proscribed all forms of secular literature that enjoyed wide circulation and provided entertainment for idle hours. In the *Christian Directory* Baxter refers his reader to an earlier work, his *Treatise of Self-Denial*, for a full discussion of harmful reading. There, in a chapter headed "False stories, romances and other tempting books," he uses the terms *romance, feigned history, love book, play book, fable* as dyslogistic epithets and treats such reading as a "point of sensuality" to be eschewed in the practice of self-denial, fol-

---

[3] Baxter, *Paraphrase on the Psalms of David* (1692), sigs. A5-A5v.
[4] Perkins, *Works*, 535.
[5] Baxter, *Christian Directory*, 61.
[6] *Ibid.*, 292.
[7] *Ibid.*, 580.

lowing the puritans who argued that plays were forbidden by the commandment against adultery. [8]

Against popular imaginative literature Baxter gives three arguments. First, it draws people away from "the great and necessary things that we all have to study," specifically from study of "the laws of God," and "those profitable treatises of divines that the world aboundeth in," all of which are necessary, or at least extremely helpful, to salvation. Second, such reading "dangerously bewitcheth and corrupteth the minds of young and empty people"; it is the "poison of youth" and "the food and work of empty, vicious, graceless persons." Third, idle books "rob men of much precious time in which much better work might be done." As Baxter elaborates the significance of this loss of time, the objection becomes progressively harder to distinguish from his first, for the "better work" that could be done turns out to be the seeking of essential knowledge, in which the treatises of divines would certainly have an important part. Thus, against popular literature, Baxter has really two arguments: the time spent reading it should be spent in religious readings instead; and by its content it corrupts the morals of the youthful and unintelligent.

Baxter did not name any of the works he condemned, perhaps because he was wise enough not to advertise his opponent's products. Many other puritans went no farther than listing the categories of harmful books, without giving examples. Their comments, like Baxter's, are useful because even their repetitions and redundancies help illustrate the tone and scope of their attacks. Thomas Goodwin condemns "playbooks, jeering pasquils, romances, feigned stories." [9] Richard Greenham, citing Ascham, finds provocations to lust in "the unchaste and wanton love songs of Italian poetry." [10] Nicholas Bownd objects particularly to the reading and singing of ballads. [11] But some puritans were more confident of their influence over readers, or more naive, and gave names to illustrate what they and others included

---

[8]Baxter, *A Treatise of Self-Denial* (1675), 157-59.
[9]Thomas Goodwin, *The Vanity of Thoughts Discovered* (1638), 26-27.
[10]Greenham, *Works*, preface.
[11]Nicholas Bownd, *Sabbathum Veteris et Novi Testamenti* (1606), 426.

in the proscribed categories. For Robert Bolton, the sign of a "fleshly memory" is its inability to retain the doctrine of salvation while it can repeat a long story about Robin Hood or Guy of Warwick. [12] Bolton's examples testify to the ineffectuality of puritan strictures, for the same works, among others, were condemned by the Elizabethan puritan, Edward Dering. Dering divides harmful books chronologically into two groups. Among stories whose vogue has passed, Dering lists "Bevis of Hampton, Guy of Warwick, Arthur of the Round Table, Huon of Bordeaux, Oliver of the Castle, the four sons of Aymon, . . . the witless devices of Gargantua, Howleglass, Aesop, Robin Hood, Adam Bell, Friar Rush, the fools of Gotham, and a thousand such other." These appealed to the English people in the dark days before the Reformation, and were comparable in folly and superstition to "their saints' lives, their tales of Robin Goodfellow." But Dering finds equally pernicious books among the favorite readings of his contemporaries: "our Songs and Sonnets, our Palaces of Pleasure, our unchaste fables and tragedies"; and he is shocked by the very titles of "the Court of Venus, the Castle of Love, and many others as shameless as these." [13] Presumably Dering would have rejected not only the whole corpus of medieval literature, but the amatory poems of the Renaissance as well, including the poetry of Shakespeare.

Dent, in the *Plain Man's Pathway*, also supplies a list of condemned books, perhaps because the exigencies of the dialogue force him to give the devil his due. His "caviller," Antilegon, tries to seduce the divine, Theologus, with a literary prescription guaranteed to drive away melancholy; the ingredients include "The Court of Venus; The Palace of Pleasure; Bevis of Southampton; Ellen of Rummin; the merry jest of the Friar and the Boy; the pleasant tale of Clem of the Clough, Adam Bell, and William of Cloudesly; the odd tale of William, Richard, and Humphrey; the pretty conceit of John Splinter's last Will and

[12]Robert Bolton, *The Carnall Professor* (1634), 94-95.
[13]*M. Derings Workes* (1614), preface to *A Brief and Necessary Catechism.* This passage is reprinted by H. R. D. Anders, "Elizabethan Popular Books and Ballads noticed by E. D., a Puritan, in 1572," *Shakespeare-Jahrbuch*, XL (1904), 229.

Testament." [14] The literary tone of Dent's list is a shade lower than that of Dering's, though both were thinking obviously of the general public. By twentieth-century standards, Beard proscribes a group of works with a higher level of quality; following Vives' argument for censorship of "unhonest songs and poems," he lists as objectionable "Amadis, Tristram, Lancelot du Lac, Melusine, Poggius' Scurrilities, and Boccace novelties." [15] A large part of the scale of literary sophistication lies between "the merry jest of the friar and the boy" and "Boccace novelties," but to the preachers the works had in common popular appeal and lack of edifying content; the people wasted their time and risked their moral and religious welfare with them.

In their censure of the romances, especially, the puritans followed the most respectable humanistic authorities. Erasmus, with typical moderation and classical orientation, found it distressing to "see many a one taking delight in the tales of Arthur and Lancelot, and other tales of similar nature which are not only about tyrants but also very poorly done, stupid, and fit to be 'old wives' tales.' " This condemnation, limited to the unprofitableness and aesthetic faults, parallels some of the puritan strictures, but Erasmus does not raise as many objections as the puritans did, and the works he recommends instead are not moral treatises of godly divines, but "the comedies or the legends of the poets," [16] which the puritans would have found profitable, with reservations, but not the ideal substitute for romances.

A more rigorous critic, and, unlike Erasmus, one much quoted by the puritans, was the younger humanist, Juan Luis Vives. His denunciation of romances, with the titles of English works added to his list of proscribed works by his English translator, is not only parallel to, but doubtless the source of, many of the puritan attacks. Objecting to "filthiness," Vives called for legal action against specific works in various countries: "in Spain, Amadise, Florisande, Tirante, Tristane, and Celestina, the baude . . .; in

---

[14]Dent, *Plain Man's Pathway*, 371.

[15]Beard, *Theatre of God's Judgments*, 149-50.

[16]Desiderius Erasmus, *The Education of a Christian Prince*, trans. Lester K. Born (New York: Columbia University Press, 1936) , 200.

France, Lancelote du Lake, Paris and Vienna, Ponthus and Sidonia, and Melucyne; in Flanders, Florys and Whyte-floure, Leonell and Canomoure, Curias and Florete, Pyramus and Thisbe." Richard Hyrde added to the list: "in England, Parthenope, Genarides, Hippomadon, William and Meliour, Libius, and Arthur, Guye, Bevis." [17]

But not only the puritans were influenced by this list. Side by side with his demonstration of a comprehensive enthusiasm for contemporary English poetry and drama, Francis Meres listed romances that were to be "censured" as "hurtfull to youth": "Amadis de Gaule, . . . Bevis of Hampton, Guy of Warwicke, Arthur of the Round Table, Huon of Burdeaux, Oliver of the Castle, The Foure Sonnes of Aymon, Gargantua, Gireleon, The Honour of Chivalrie, Primaleon of Greece, Palmerin de Oliva, the Seven Champions, The Myrror of Knighthood, Blancherdine, Mervin, Howleglasse, The Stories of Palladyne and Palmendos, The Blacke Knight, the Maiden Knight, The History of Caelestina, The Castle of Fame, Gallian of France, Ornatus and Artesia." [18] Such examples make clear that in the humanistic tradition, Ascham's famous denunciation of the *"Morte Arthure,* the whole pleasure of which book standeth in two special points, in open manslaughter and bold bawdry," is noteworthy only for the sharpness of its phrasing. The rest of Ascham's criticism is just as apposite here, though less often quoted: "In which book those be counted the noblest knights that do kill most men without any quarrel, and commit foulest adulteries by subtlest shifts: as Sir Launcelote, with the wife of King Arthure, his master; Sir Tristram, with the wife of King Marke, his

[17]Juan Luis Vives, *A very fruteful and pleasant book called the Instruction of a Christen Woman,* trans. Rycharde Hyrde (1557), sig. D2v. The passage is quoted in *Vives and the Renascence Education of Women,* ed. Foster Watson (London: Edward Arnold, 1912), 59. For one estimate of Vives' influence on later strictures against romances, see R. S. Crane, "The Vogue of *Guy of Warwick* from the Close of the Middle Ages to the Romantic Revival," *Publications of the Modern Language Association,* XXX (1915), 137-38.

[18]Francis Meres, *Palladis Tamia* (1598). See *Elizabethan Critical Essays,* ed. G Gregory Smith (2 vols., London: Oxford University Press, 1904), II, 308-309.

uncle; Sir Lamerocke, with the wife of King Lote, that was his own aunt." [19]

From a general, unequivocal condemnation of romances and amatory poems, which humanists such as Ascham and Vives also disliked, to an attack on poetry as an art is a long distance, which the puritans did not attempt to traverse. Frequently, however, they seem to have taken long steps away from Renaissance humanism. In the quotations given above, the word "feigned" appears regularly as a pejorative term indicating that the puritans thought of fiction not as an imaginative view of reality, but as simple falsehood. This, of course, is the view against which Sidney argued. The same attitude shows up more clearly in the use of the words "poet" and "poetical" as though they had unfavorable connotations. For instance, Joseph Caryl speaks of "poetical raptures" and "feigned romances" as synonymous with falsehood, as distortions of and antitheses to the reality of history. [20] John Goodwin, arguing for the patent truth of scriptural representations, points out that "the hell of poets" is "a hell to play and make sport withall," not a place to fear, and that its descriptions are "at mere peradventure and poetlike, so as more to delight the fancy, than to strike or trouble the consciences of men." [21] No one, of course, would have ascribed to poetry the truth and force of the Bible; but above and beyond the platitudinous argument, Goodwin's tone shows some contempt for the work of the poetic imagination. The contempt can be discounted partially, but not entirely explained away, by knowledge that scorn for the truth, and even for the didactic and formative value, of any works that exigency or expediency of argument brought up for comparison with the Bible was common to humanists and puritans alike.

If Goodwin had little respect for the poet's hell, Beard was ready enough to assume a real hell as the destiny of many poets. To students of literature, the most interesting passage in his *Theatre of God's Judgments* is the biographically important

---

[19] Smith, *Elizabethan Critical Essays*, I, 4.
[20] Caryl, *England's Plus Ultra*, sig. A2.
[21] John Goodwin, *The Divine Authority of the Scriptures Asserted* (1648), 83.

account of Marlowe's death. The estimate of Marlowe's character is unfavorable; he was one "Marlin, by profession a scholar, brought up from his youth in the university of Cambridge, but by practice a play-maker and a poet of scurrility." [22] Since the word "poet" is qualified by the phrase "of scurrility," and otherwise Marlowe is denounced mainly for blasphemy and atheism, the passage is not an attack on poetry. Later in his *Theatre* Beard exhibits some "wanton and lewd poets" who committed suicide, including "Labienus, the railing poet," "Lucretius, the atheist," "Empedocles, the vainglorious poet," Silius Italicus, and "Cornelius Gallus, an amatorious poet." [23] In context, the suicides are God's judgments against sin. Again poetry as such is not attacked directly, but the list of doomed and damned poets is extensive and varied enough to show that the poet was suspect, that he was likely to be called wanton and lewd without scrupulous regard to the appropriateness of the epithets.

A general, often vaguely based suspicion of the art of poetry marked the furthest advance of the puritan attack on literature as an art. It could not be utterly condemned under any circumstances, because the writers of Scripture themselves had used it. But that basic, incontrovertible fact had ambivalent meanings for the puritan attitude toward any literature besides the Bible. We have seen that the stylistic merits of scriptural writings had various implications for the puritan theory of style; while some puritans thought the writers of Scripture the examples to be followed and urged a grave and sober eloquence, others contended that all human rhetoric was vain and even impious when compared with such artistry, that it was best to write and speak plainly, leaving a monopoly of eloquence to the Holy Spirit. The reactions to the poetry of the Bible, considered as artistic achievement, were similarly varied. To some, all human attempts at emulation were useless, because however far poetic skill might carry the author, he lacked the divine inspiration that gave form as well as truth to the Psalms, the Song of Solomon, and Ecclesiastes. Here was not only the best poetry, but its divine,

---

[22] Beard, *Theatre of God's Judgments*, 149-50.
[23] *Ibid.*, 315.

pristine archetype, of which the pagan classics were only distorted reflections and adulterated imitations. But others saw in the poetry of the Bible a sanction for human poetry. To them, it was fitting and proper to· emulate the prophets, although, of course, no one could duplicate the achievement, the Word being *sui generis*. But as the preacher served God commendably when he interpreted Scripture, clothed it in his own words, and put it into a form he had devised, so the poet could profitably and honestly use his talents and the resources of poetic tradition to embody his vision of the truth. Human literature was thus both exalted and humbled by the poetry of the Bible.

The ambivalent attitude at first glance may seem a convenient pattern for classifying puritan views of poetry. But the puritans did not apply to literary questions the rigid logic that characterized them in ecclesiastical disputes; they did not often reason deliberately from their literary premises to a conclusion. Both attitudes are sometimes expressed by one person on different occasions; and even where a definition of an individual's attitude is possible, one usually discovers a compromise. The effect for literature was the development of varied attitudes under various specific stimuli.

One effect was the writing and use of psalm paraphrases in verse. Some argued that a paraphrase was legitimate only if it was prose—even prosaic—and rendered the doctrine as literally as possible. But the puritan substitute for liturgical music, psalm-singing, required metrical translation; and even though poetic values generally yielded to doctrinal considerations, the use of meter was the sanction of a poetic device and thus, for most puritans, a limited acceptance of poetry. In fact, the psalms were often intended to displace secular ballads in the affections of the common people. By giving them this function, the puritans tacitly acknowledged a similarity, or at least an analogy, in aesthetic appeal. Nicholas Bownd saw a natural rivalry between ballads and psalms, even though he would have called it a mutual repugnance. He notes that when "the light of the gospel came first in, the singing of ballads . . . began to cease." But subsequently, a revival of ballad-singing made him fear that it

might "drive away the singing of psalms." [24] Baxter argued, in
effect, that the devil had used the charm of poetry in secular
ballads to seduce men. The metrical paraphrases were, for him,
an attempt to give men poetry and song without the unwhole-
some effect of the ballads—in fact, to consecrate poetry to the
service of religion. [25]

Whenever conclusions were drawn about the poetic quality of
psalms and other Biblical writings, the Bible was subjected in
greater or lesser degree to critical literary analysis. It was only
logical, then, that puritan rhetoricians should turn to the Bible
for illustrations of tropes and other rhetorical devices. One of
the consequences of their scriptural orientation is illustrated by
John Smith's *Mystery of Rhetoric Unveiled.* Essentially it is a
handbook of rhetoric using the Bible, along with Sidney's
prose, as a source of examples. As a major aim of his work,
Smith emphasizes its value for interpreting the Bible properly,
for teaching the reader to understand various types of metaphor-
ical expressions, to distinguish figurative from nonfigurative expressions, and, in general, to get at the meaning of a passage
by recognizing its form. But Smith's work merely serves religion;
it is not a religious work, and it even has an important secular
and literary aim. The author hopes that "this work will . . . be
useful and advantageous to youth and others, enabling them
to find out the elegancy in any author, and likewise help the invention of learners, who may beautify a speech, and adorn a discourse with elocution, by drawing their discourse through the
several tropes and figures, and taking what may best befit their
purposes." [26] Thus Smith, by fulfilling the pious aim of substi-

---

[24] Bownd, *Sabbathum Veteris et Novi Testamenti,* 426.

[25] Baxter, *Paraphrase on the Psalms of David* (1692), sig. A5v.

[26] John Smith, *The Mysterie of Rhetorique unvail'd* (1657), preface. Smith
identifies himself as a resident of Montague Close, Southwark. The attribu-
tion of this book by Wing (*Short-Title Catalogue, 1641-1700*) to John Ser-
geant, a Roman Catholic controversialist, seems unlikely. Whatever Smith's
religious position, the book carries the laudatory imprimatur of the puritan
licenser, Joseph Caryl. Other writers who made similar, if not so extensive,
use of the Bible are Dudley Fenner, John Barton, and Thomas Hall. See
Foster Watson, *The English Grammar Schools to 1660* (Cambridge: Cambridge University Press, 1908), 450.

tuting the Bible for the usual pagan sources of rhetorical ex-
empla, was forced to proceed by examining Biblical language
according to artistic criteria, and ended by sanctioning, in effect, a secular, literary attitude toward the Bible.

The same ambivalent result, with its effect of bridging the
gap between religion and literature, even of integrating religious
and secular writings into one corpus of literature with a common
didactic function and a common set of evaluatory criteria, was
achieved even more easily with religious works of puritan authors. As usual, the motivating impulse was the attempt to displace secular writings, with their questionable moral effects, by
works of sound morality and unimpeachable didactic efficacy.
Another John Smith illustrates the attempt by putting his sermons into competition with tales, interludes, and ballads. He
published his sermons in answer to his rhetorical question, "Why
should the stationer's shops and some men's shelves contain nothing but Guy of Warwick, William of Cloudesly, Skeggins, and
Wolner's jests, and writings of like quality?" [27] The implied relationship may seem incongruous, but the attitude behind it
was ubiquitous.

Usually, however, the aim to capture the audience of the secular press was not so explicitly stated. Often it appears as the logical premise underlying the use of terms borrowed from poets
and writers of prose fiction to describe a work. For instance,
Daniel Rogers calls his *Practical Catechism* the "whole posy of
the flowers herein bound together." [28] The posy, of course, con-
sisted of doctrinal and moral precepts instead of the poems
usually advertised under that name. The writer of the preface
to Reynolds' *Meditations on the fall and rising of Peter* called
the work "An Iliad in a nutshell." [29] And Lewis Bayly, in his
Practice of Piety, resorted to dramatic theory to warn and encourage his reader: "Be not discouraged . . . at the harshness of
the beginning; but look for smoother matter in the middest, and
most smooth in the perclose and wind-up of all. For this dialogue

---

[27] John Smith (the Se-baptist, d. 1612), ep. ded. to *Bright Morning Star*,
quoted by Haller, *Rise of Puritanism*, 183, 390.

[28] Daniel Rogers, *A Practicall Catechisme* (1640), preface.

[29] Reynolds, *Works*, IV, 6.

nath in it, not the nature of a tragedy, which is begun with joy
and ended with sorrow, but a comedy, which is begun with sorrow and endeth with joy." [30] Doubtless Bayly saw in his work
a divine comedy if it led his readers to salvation. For him and
for many others, the aim was to replace poetry and fiction with
sounder morality, but in the attempt they exalted and sanctioned
the arts they were pre-empting for their religious ends.

The indirect expressions of respect for poetry are significant
because they, more clearly than direct statements, show the
pervasiveness of puritan esteem for the literary arts, not because
more direct statements are not available. From first to last the
puritans made a distinction between popular literature and what
they considered good literature. [31] They saw it, in fact, as a distinction between idle amusements and what could truly be
called literature. A good example is Whitlock's argument that
young people should not waste their time "reading romances"
but should devote it to "the study of good literature." [32] Whitlock does not define his terms, but very likely he expresses the
attitude that Perkins phrased metaphorically. Condemning as
"evil talk" all "vain love-songs, ballads, interludes, and amorous
books," Perkins qualifies and limits his strictures: "This is the
thing we are to shun in the reading of poets, yet so, as mariners
do in navigation, who forsake not the sea, but decline and fly
from the rocks." [33] Nor was the distinction understood only by
casuists; it was clear enough to Lucy Hutchinson, who perhaps
could not have stated it as a principle. She confessed apologetically that during her precocious but naive childhood she
"thought it no sin to learn or hear witty songs and amorous
sonnets and poems," but she writes proudly of her poem wh
set to music, first brought her the appreciative notice of

---

[30] Lewis Bayly, *The Practice of Pietie* (1633), sig. A3v.

[31] It is in connection with this literature that one can speak of "the honor
in which they [the puritans] held the poet's high office," Miller and Johnson,
The Puritans, 547. The term *good literature* apparently derives from
Cicero's *bonae literae* and is analogous to *belles-lettres*; on this point see
Morison, *Intellectual Life of Colonial New England*, 32.

[32] John Whitlock, *The Upright Man and His Happy End* (1658), 38-39.
This work is a funeral sermon for Francis Pierrepont.

[33] Perkins, *Works*, 60.

Hutchinson. [34] In the after-glow of the puritan era, Baxter, who had uncompromisingly denounced romances, suggests that young men under twenty, should read, among other things, the poets, whom he classifies with philosophers and orators under "Scholastical History." Baxter does not include any poets in his lists of works essential to personal libraries of various sizes, but he indicates clearly enough that his bibliographies are not exclusive and elsewhere, as we shall see, he does recommend some poets. [35]

Knowledge of "good literature" reflected credit upon a minister. It was one of the merits extolled at his death, when, according to one puritan tradition in the funeral sermon, he was described as an example for the living. Gataker, whose comment on Richard Stock's style has been quoted, also praised Stock for his "singular proficiency in those studies of humanity that are as handmaids to divinity," and his ability to "entertwine piety and humanity." [36] Since he was a literary scholar, Gataker would be expected to praise humanistic studies, but his view was representative. In turn, Simeon Ashe, in his funeral sermon on Gataker, noted that the scholar-preacher's "polite literature was admired by the great lights of learning abroad" and that "he made his human literature . . . become subservient to religion." [37] The position of handmaid to divinity may not appear sufficiently exalted to a critic in the Romantic tradition, but no Renaissance theorist would have placed any human art or achievement on a higher level of esteem.

In the seventeenth-century controversy over the value of human learning, poetry was given relatively favorable treatment. The opponent of the universities, John Webster, granted that it had

---

[34]Lucy Hutchinson, *Memoirs of the Life of Colonel Hutchinson*, ed. Rev. Julius Hutchinson (5th ed., London, 1846), 18, 57-58.

[35]Baxter, *Christian Directory*, 918, 922. Puritan bibliographies generally include only religious works. For another famous example, see Hugh Peters, *A Dying Fathers Last Legacy to an Onely Child* (1660); this work is discussed by J. Max Patrick, *Hugh Peters, A Study in Puritanism* (Buffalo: University of Buffalo Studies, 1946), 191, and by Raymond Phineas Stearns, *The Strenuous Puritan, Hugh Peter* (Urbana: University of Illinois Press, 1954), 422.

[36]Gataker, *Abraham's Decease*, 3.

[37]Ashe, *Gray Hayres Crowned with Grace* (1655), 55.

some utility, like oratory or rhetoric, and merely warned that such studies should not consume too much time. Though "ornamental," these arts are useful as the shell is to a kernel. Webster discouraged the writing of poetry as an academic exercise, citing the Platonic theory of poetic inspiration as a "divine afflation," by which the poet is mastered and directed. Thus "eloquence and poesy" are "gifts of nature," not disciplines. If the implications of this theory seem negative, Webster, who was ready to proscribe much, at least allowed "every man to the freedom of his own genius" in the use of poetry and rhetoric. [38]

For most of the puritans, Webster's caution against the writing of poetry was superfluous. They rarely quoted Plato, but frequently enough they repeated or paraphrased the commonplace quoted by Webster, *nascitur, non fit poeta.* Yet, ironically, they often used it in apologies for their verses, and paralleled it with assertions of an overarching didactic or religious aim, seeking to explain and excuse their deficiency in poetic talent. Here also they showed their respect for poetry, for they apologized not so much for having written poems as for not having written them well. The most direct statement justifying poetic composition was made by Gataker, who allowed the practice to ministers. Accused by John Saltmarsh, whose mystical obscurantism made him a more intransigent enemy of the arts than all but a few of his contemporaries, of being "comical and poetical" in his old age, contrary to decorum, Gataker defends the right of any minister to "exercise his poetry, if he have a vein that way . . . and that in old age too, as many worthy and religious persons have done." For himself, Gataker professes lack of talent. He too believes that poets are not made but born, and he disclaims possession of natural genius, but he emphasizes the lack of validity in Saltmarsh's criticism, not the inapplicability of the criticism to him. [39]

The criticism could have been applied more relevantly to a man whom one would believe much less inclined by his circumstances and general interests to write poetry. The Devonshire

---

[38]John Webster, *Academiarum Examen* (1654), 21, 89, 108.
[39]Gataker, *Shadowes without Substance* (1646), 4.

preacher, Samuel Hieron, who consistently defended the plain style, excused his verses on the grounds that he was fighting fire with fire. A certain "Popish rime" was circulating in the western counties, and had influenced many of the "simple-seduced"; therefore, Hieron explains, "I have endeavored to make the lettuce like the lips (as the proverb is) and to proportion myself like unto him in versing." Writing a poem is a difficult task that Hieron has assumed because of his sense of duty. His apology for the quality of his verse is traditional and inevitable; he believes that a poet is born, and that, as Ovid wrote, leisure is a prerequisite for poetic composition: "You will wonder, I am sure (considering my profession) to see me become a poet, and indeed, I do almost marvel at it myself, knowing myself to want the two principal furtherances of poetry: the one is nature's instinct, which God in his providence hath denied me; the other is a certain retired freedom from all such business which may breed distraction." [40]

Hieron's poem was not his only departure from the standard forms of the sermon and expository treatise. His apology for writing a dialogue is less extensive and shows less uneasiness about a breach of decorum, but his excuse is the same, the didactic efficacy of the form: "I have trodden in an old beaten path, both by old and new writers, by divines and heathen, namely to frame my matter to the form of a dialogue, a very good way (in my seeming) to help the understanding of common men." [41] The dialogue, in fact, hardly needed vindication; Dent, instead of excusing his use of the rhetorical form, uses the form to excuse the presentation of unorthodox views and pagan quotations, which appear in the speeches of his protagonists: "Remember," he cautions, "that I am in a dialogue, not in a sermon." [42] Dent apparently took for granted what Hieron explained, that a dialogue could be more clear and intelligible than a sermon; but both certainly knew that it was a secular art form. The basic justification was the same for the dialogue and the moral poem. Though Hieron did not say it explicitly, he, like many

[40]Hieron, *Works*, ep. ded. to *An Answer to a Popish Rime*.
[41]*Ibid.*, preface to *A Preacher's Plea*.
[42]Dent, *Plain Man's Pathway*, sig. A3.

other puritans, was trying to ornament his doctrine to make it more attractive. Ultimately, puritan ministers who attempted verses or dialogues had as their implied motto Horace's *omne tulit punctum qui miscuit utile dulci.*

The example of the Bible, the need to compete with ballads and romances, the didactic value of combining the useful with the sweet—all were cited or implied at times to justify the use of literary artistry. But as one reads the prefaces and explanations, he cannot help wondering to what degree they may have been rationalizations of a genuine aesthetic feeling. The cumulative effect of all the apologies for adopting secular forms and techniques is to give the impression that the creative instinct of the preacher had simply overflowed its usual channels and poured itself into half-consciously prepared forms. And one comes close to an admission that the form of a work was dictated by the author's self-indulgence of artistic creativity in Richard Bernard's preface to his allegorical *Isle of Man.* The professed aim is quite "puritanical": to exhibit the wretchedness of man's estate and to point out the way to salvation. Therefore, Bernard must account for his use of allegory and humor, not only as tolerable per se, but as appropriate to his sober theme. In traditional puritan manner, Bernard seeks Biblical examples to justify his practice, citing Nathan, Isaiah, and Ezekiel for his use of allegory and Abraham and Job for the use of "smiling and joyful laughter . . . which may stand with sober gravity." Then, perhaps in a moment of naive abandon, Bernard comes closer to expressing a more general motive than more self-conscious and judicious puritans ever approached, though like them he keeps his eyes focused on the Bible: "Well, I have clothed this book as it is; it may be some humor took me, as once it did old Jacob, who apparalled Joseph differently from all the rest of his brethren in a parti-colored coat." And like old Jacob, he prefers this late offspring to his earlier. [43]

Equally honest and much more detailed is Baxter's preface to his *Poetical Fragments.* [44] His discussion of poetry is especially significant because of the vigor of his attack on plays,

[43]Bernard, *The Isle of Man* (1627), preface.
[44]Baxter, *Poetical Fragments* (1681), preface.

romances, and the other popular secular literature of his and earlier times. It shows that a puritan could reject Guy of Warwick and still enthusiastically admire Herbert, Sandys, and even Cowley; and it illustrates the discriminating appreciation of poetic effects that could accompany an insistence that the engrossing concern of man is his salvation. Baxter's immediate task in the preface is to account for the writing of his poems. He admits that they are submitted to the public because of "passion"—that is, in this instance, impulsive feeling—rather than judgment, but he tries to justify the passion. His esteem for poetry, which he does not bother to distinguish clearly from music, is unqualified. Professing amazement at the "learned, discreet men" who "know not what a tune is," he suggests that they must suffer from a constitutional defect. Of his own attitude, he writes, "I confess that harmony and melody are the pleasure and elevation of my soul." The insistent references to sound are important, for they indicate that Baxter responded strongly and sensitively to rhythmic, tonal, and other aesthetic effects in poetry, not solely to its message. In context, it is his sensitive aesthetic perception that projects his exclamation, "Sure there is something of heaven in holy poetry. It charmeth souls into loving harmony and concord."

His own poetry is offered to the reader with the traditional humility and apologies. He has not changed his lifelong opinion that a painter, a musician, and a poet are "contemptible if they be not excellent," nor does he believe that his poems have technical merits; instead, he has come to believe that even artistically defective poetry may have its uses. He has published his verses because of the several didactic ends they may serve; he believes, "1. That being fitted to women and vulgar wits, which are the far greatest number, they may be useful to such, though contemptible to those of higher elevation and expectation. 2. And being suited to afflicted, sick, dying, troubled, sad, and doubting persons, the number of which is so great in these calamitous times, may render them useful to more than I desire." No preacher could have taken exception to the thoroughgoing didacticism of this aim, but no preacher would have objected to

Baxter's poetry on moral grounds. His defense is addressed to
people with sophisticated taste in literature, who might object
on technical grounds to the artistic quality of his verse. Hence,
his apology is a tribute to the literary arts.

The preface is doubly valuable because of the critical opinions
Baxter gives of specific poets. It is, by date of publication, a
Restoration document, but the poets named lead one back, like
Baxter's religious tenets, through the era of puritan rule to the
very beginnings of the seventeenth century. And the evaluations
take one forward to modern critics, who would find little to
reject in them. He considers "Lady Katherine Phillips" the best
of the women poets. His reaction to "Honest George Wither . . .
a rustic poet" is typically puritan in its esteem, but simultaneously modern, as Baxter condescendingly remarks the lack of polish in many of his verses. [45] His estimate of Cowley as first for
"strength of his wit" is typical of his age, though acceptable only
in a very special and not laudatory sense today. Among other
poets, Baxter lists Quarles, Fulke Greville, Davies, Sylvester as
translator of Du Bartas, Sandys, and Herbert, the last three being
his favorites. The gross over-rating of Sylvester is typical of the
earlier seventeenth century; even Milton may have been guilty
of it, to a degree. Typical also is his evaluation of Sandys, whose
"excellent and elegant" paraphrases of the Bible meet with only
one objection: they are too difficult for the common man to
understand readily. Here Baxter seems more judicious than
later critics, though perhaps only a theory of literary history
that denies translations a place in the corpus of a nation's literature keeps Sandys, like Fairfax, from being considered a significant English poet. But Baxter's comment on George Herbert
shows the keenest perception of artistic effects in poetry. In spite
of his deference to Cowley's reputation, Baxter's aesthetic sense
leads him to a surer judgment than many sophisticated critics
of his time attained: "I know that Cowley and others far excel

---

[45]Here Baxter's opinion has clearly stood the test of time. It is quoted,
along with a phrase from Charles Lamb, as almost a definition of Wither's
tone and appeal by Douglas Bush, *English Literature in the Earlier Seventeenth Century, 1600-1660* (Oxford: Clarendon Press, 1946), 82.

Herbert in wit and accurate composure. But as Seneca takes with me above all his contemporaries, because he speaketh things by words, feelingly and seriously, like a man that is past jest, so Herbert speaks to God like one that really believeth a God, and whose business in the world is most with God." [46]

Though Baxter's evaluations are not finely articulated, the few words he devotes to each poet are aptly chosen; they not only sum up the quality of the verse, but also demonstrate the sensitivity of Baxter's taste. In his comparison of Herbert and Cowley he discriminates carefully between mere artfulness and depth of religious feeling. Yet his criterion is as much literary as moral, for he praises in Herbert the effect of sincerity rather than the sincerity itself. In general Baxter's practical criticism testifies to extensive reading in poetry, during which aesthetic perceptions were not overwhelmed by his moral and religious preoccupations; and whatever his own poetry may have been, he thought of a poem as more than a verse paraphrase of an edifying message. Finally, and perhaps this is most important, his criticism shows that a puritan could reject poetry when it served as popular amusement and yet retain his esteem for poetry as an art.

---

[46] Concerning Herbert's good reputation among the puritans see F. E. Hutchinson's introduction to his edition of *The Works of George Herbert* (Oxford: Clarendon Press, 1945), xliv. Thomas Hall and Peter Sterry were among the admirers of Herbert's poems.

CHAPTER 5

As the Heathen Man Sayeth

NOTWITHSTANDING their universal rejection of the theatre and romances and ballads, the puritans made no concerted attack on the Muses. Thalia, Erato, and Terpsichore (taken in the Renaissance view of their functions) seemed inimical to the welfare of the souls under their charge, but even the first two of these, along with their more aristocratic sisters, were welcome in the puritan minister's study, where they were called upon to help in religious controversy, as Hieron's example shows. or to assist in comforting the afflicted, as Baxter purposed in his verses. They were, of course, omnipresent in the schools, where puritans and conservative Anglicans alike studied Latin and Greek in the standard classical poets. They encountered some objections there, but usually the question was paganism, not artistic vanity or immorality. Even then, the objection was generally not against use of the pagans, but against failure to use Christian authors as well, against an exclusively pagan curriculum. Gataker protested, in a rhetorical question, "What difference will there be between a Christian parent and an heathen, a Christian schoolmaster and a pagan, if the parent or schoolmaster teach his children and scholars matters of civility and human learning alone?" [1] But, like most puritans, Gataker thought the pagan authors indispensable for the study of languages, and his view constitutes a sort of puritan *via media*.

The main objections to the pagans were aroused by the falseness of their religion. However, it may be well to recall here

---

[1] Gataker, *Certain Sermons*, 16.

that in the Renaissance view the pagans did not use a theology wholly and utterly distinct from the Christian, at least not in its origins. Pagan religious beliefs, as well as the rest of pagan philosophy and arts and sciences, had been derived originally from the truth revealed to Adam and later to Moses. Thus all pagan knowledge and art were corruptions of the truth, not simple falsehood, and contained some glimmerings and shadows of truth, even of Christianity. This notion, which Theophilus Gale documented extensively in his *Court of the Gentiles* (1669-1678) was ubiquitous, and although the puritans do not insist upon it, they could not have escaped its influence.

Some of the uses made of pagan writers will occasion no surprise. When John Goodwin finds evidence for the truth of Scripture among pagan poets, and cites analogues to the Biblical account of the creation in Hesiod, Sophocles, Aeschylus, Plato, Empedocles, and others, he writes in an honorable tradition of Christian apologetics; he employs pagan authorities logically, inevitably, and irreproachably. [2] Similarly, Perkins cites Homer and Plato as pagan witnesses to the truth of the Biblical account of the creation, and Virgil on the existence of a redeemer. [3] But almost as frequent, and in some ways directly in contrast with that conscious and deliberate use of pagan authorities, is the spontaneous appearance of classical phrases and references woven inextricably into the texture of puritan writing. For instance, Thomas Hall writes in controversy that "if every Phaeton that thinks himself able may drive the chariot of the sun, no wonder if the world be set on fire." [4] Doubtless Hall wrote unreflectingly, and probably none of his readers, unless we posit an eagle-eyed Samuel How, were conscious that the statement could be in any way incongruous in a book about the high office of the preacher.

At one extreme, objections were raised against the moral content of pagan classics; fears were expressed that along with excellent diction the student might acquire dubious moral notions. For instance, Rainolds quotes Augustine to the effect that "he

[2]Goodwin, *Divine Authority of the Scriptures*, 373.
[3]Perkins, *Arte of Prophecying*, 21-22.
[4]Thomas Hall, *The Pulpit Guarded* (1650), 13.

learned many profitable words in vain, poetical fancies; but
such as . . . may be learned in things not vain." Questioning the
moral effect of Terence, Rainolds quotes Vives in favor of the
expurgation of classical authors in books for children. [5] Yet,
other puritans continued to read Terence and other pagans without a twinge of conscience. At the other extreme from Rainolds
was Richard Bernard, who blandly and cheerfully recommended
Terence as a moral and useful author, calling him, "a comical
poet, pithy, pleasant, and very profitable; as merry as Eutrapeles,
as grave as Cato, as ethical as Plato; he can play craftily the
cozener, and cunningly the clown; he will tell you the nature
of the fraudulent flatterer, the grim and greedy old sire, the
roisting ruffian, the mincing minion and beastly bawd, that in
telling truth by these figments, men might become wise to avoid
such vices, and learn to practice virtue, which was Terence's
purpose in setting of these comedies forth in Latin, mine in
translating them into English." [6] We may doubt the accuracy
of this explanation of Terence's and Bernard's purposes, but the
statements are commonplace in Renaissance apologetics for
classical literature. Even if Bernard's account of motives is lack-
ing in scrupulosity or candor, he shows how the puritans were
able to justify the reading of classical authors to their own satisfaction.

Because of their education, the puritan preachers were thoroughly saturated with classical learning, including poetry and
drama. Vernacular literature, of course, was not a respectable
academic subject, though Baxter's example is evidence that the
puritans could acquire an extensive extra-curricular familiarity

---

[5] John Rainolds, *Th' overthrow of Stage-Playes* (Middelburgh, 1600), 123.
Augustine's famous reference to his boyish response to Virgil was often
quoted: "I was compelled to learn about the wanderings of a certain Aeneas,
oblivious of my own wanderings, and to weep for Dido dead, who slew her-
self for love. And all this while I bore with dry eyes my own wretched self
dying to thee, O God, my life, in the midst of these things." See Augustine,
Confessions and Enchiridion, trans. Albert C. Outler (Philadelphia: The
Westminster Press, 1955), 42 (Bk. I, Ch. XIII). Augustine's statement har-
monizes perfectly with many puritan references to classical literature.
[6] Bernard, *Terence in English* (1641), ep. ded. Bernard's work was a "popular school edition of Terence," according to Donald L. Clark, *John Milton
at St. Paul's School* (New York: Columbia University Press, 1948), 174.

with it. Polite literature thus figured in puritan everyday life appreciably. But did it enter even the pulpit, where its presence would have signified its approval as a highly trusted and useful handmaid of divinity and would have gained it the highest respect among the puritan citizens of England? Contemporary poetry did not achieve this distinction. Since preachers looked upon the sermon as a literary genre in itself, perhaps other contemporary literature was excluded by their notion of literary decorum, even when it was admissible on didactic grounds. Whatever the reason, quotations from and allusions to contemporary English poets are practically absent from the sermons and moral treatises of the puritans. Grosart cited some allusions to Shakespeare in the works of Sibbes, but the evidence is not convincing. For instance, Sibbes's "all is but acting a part" may be an allusion to "all the world's a stage," but no indebtedness can be proved by a similarity so general and vague. [7]

Classical poetry, however, got a different reception. Here the puritans showed considerable variations both in theory and in practice; in the theories of several, Greek and Latin quotations were permissible with restrictions. The quotation was chosen presumably for its moral content, but in practice, aptness of expression was a determining, though incidental, factor that brought literary considerations into the inner sanctum of puritan didacticism. Chracteristically, the puritans cited Biblical examples for the use of pagan literature; and, as on many other questions, St. Paul provided the necessary sanction. His rejection of the "enticing words of man's wisdom" was a deterrent to the use of any human art or learning in sermons, but it was qualified by his practice, especially by his use of Aratus in Acts 17:28, of Menander in I Corinthians 15:33, and of Epimenides in Titus 1:12, the last with the comment, "this witness is true." The three passages formed the basis of all puritan theory on the subject; they provided a franchise for the use of pagan literature, and an obstacle that required considerable ingenuity of those who would remove it to prohibit such use.

Hieron took a middle ground in restricting the use of pagan

---

[7] Sibbes, *Works*, IV, 52, 58; see also V, 232, 247-48.

quotations in sermons. In his dialogue *The Preacher's Plea*, the minister, Epaphras, first approves quotation of the Fathers, partly because "many grave, godly, and well-learned men" do it, partly because it is useful in controversy with those who claim the support of the Fathers for their opinions. Then, passing on to a more difficult question, he turns to the Bible: "For the speeches and sentences of profane authors, to bar them utterly out of sermons I dare not, because I find them used by that worthy Paul three several times." The permission seems reluctant, and the minister promptly restricts some of the freedom he has allowed: "As Paul's example warranteth, so it limiteth the use of such testimonies." In fact, the uses are limited to two: "to convince atheists and irreligious persons," and "to shame those who profess themselves Christians" by citing relevant moral or pious sentiments and examples among the heathen. The discussion ends with a caution against frequent or ostentatious use of pagan quotations. [8] At first glance the limitations appear to be stringent, but on closer examination, the second approved use—to shame Christians—appears broad and general enough to allow assiduous quoting of the moralists of Greece and Rome and numerous citations of pagan virtue. And so it often turned out in practice.

A stricter theory was developed by Thomas Taylor. In his *Commentary on Titus*, Taylor derived from Paul's use of Epimenides the doctrine that "it is not simply unlawful to allege the saying of a profane man in a sermon." But as is characteristic of puritan theory in many fields, Taylor stated a liberal principle only to hedge it with so many qualifications that almost no one could take advantage of it in practice. Like Hieron, he finds two general uses for pagan quotations, but the "shaming of Christians" with examples of pagan virtue is not one of them; pagans are to be quoted only for grammatical and linguistic reasons (to establish the meanings of words, phrases, and sentences), and to convince the pagans of their errors by using their own authorities against them. Furthermore, restrictions are placed on the manner in which the quotations may be used: they

---

[8] Hieron, *Works*, 532-33.

must be "rare and sparing"; they "must be used soberly, without affectation"; and "they may not be used to prove points of doctrine or manners," which must always be derived from Scripture. The words that have met these exacting specifications may yet find themselves with no place to go, for Taylor also restricts the occasions on which they may be used: they may not be used in sermons before church congregations, only in conferences, disputations, and "personal epistles"; they may not be addressed to Christians, only to heathen; and they should not appear frequently in one sermon. [9] In other words, they may be used only in circumstances almost identical with those in which Paul used them. Since these circumstances occurred rarely in the England of the puritans, Taylor's doctrine, when fully articulated, in effect prohibited the use of classical allusions and quotations in the writings of his contemporaries.

But Taylor was unusually rigorous. Starkly opposing views were held by some theorists who took more seriously a principle stated by Taylor himself: "All truth is the Lord's." Reynolds, in his funeral sermon on John Langley, cited Paul's three pagan allusions and also the religious use made by David of the spoils of war against the Gentiles to justify the religious use of all kinds of pagan learning. For Reynolds, the end largely justified the means, and secular writing was good whenever it could be made to serve as a handmaid to divinity. The paramount importance of the aim dictated his restrictions, which deal solely with the manner in which learning is to be employed. "Caution" seems to be his watchword; human learning should be used "not unnecessarily," "not vaingloriously," "not proudly," "not heretically," and "not profanely," but "with humility, moderation, sobriety, as a handmaid to Christ." [10]

A theory similar to Reynolds' directed Gataker's extensive use of classical learning. With a somewhat paradoxical humility, Gataker pleads the fact that he "was never furnished with any store of rhetorical lights" as his excuse "to embellish my writings

---

[9]Taylor, *A Commentarie upon the Epistle of S. Paul written to Titus* (1612), 242-44.

[10]Reynolds, *Works*, V, 32-41.

with such borrowed helps as my poor reading affordeth either out of holy or human writers." For the human writers he finds Biblical warrant in the passages traditionally cited in this context: their "speeches and observations also, either as Egyptian spoils, or as Canaanitish captives, either having passed the fire, and been purged of their heathenish dross, or being trimmed and pared from their paganish superfluities, may well and warrantably upon good grounds, even from the practice of God's spirit, be not only admitted into the commonwealth of Israel, but applied also to the use of the sanctuary and of God's service therein." [11] Far from being an ostentation of learning, his pagan helps partially compensate for his lack of artfulness. If Gataker's argument seems to us like rationalization, it was reasonable enough to the puritans, and it did his reputation no harm.

Although the range of answers was extremely wide on the basic question whether use of the pagan writers was lawful and proper in sermons and treatises, even greater divergences appeared when distinctions were made between the oral and the printed discourse. All varieties of learning were more readily admitted into writing than into preaching. Undoubtedly, rhetorical effectiveness was the criterion; in a preached sermon quotations and other lore might distract or confuse the reader and impede the flow of thought, whereas in a book they could be passed over or studied at leisure, as the reader saw fit. But the difference is not always explained in this way. Henry Holland apparently held a theory of decorum in style which made quotation of Greek and Latin authors proper only in writings. Addressing himself to the reader who had heard Greenham preach, Holland accounts for the Greek and Latin quotations "which thou couldest never hear in his preaching," by saying that Greenham "ever sought to preach Christ and not his own gifts." [12] The distinction is not presented logically, and probably it arises not from logic, but from a mixture of theory and custom; Holland and others believed that frequent quotation was an ostentation of learning, but they were so accustomed to seeing quotations in

[11] Gataker, *Certain Sermons*, ep. ded.
[12] Greenham, *Works*, preface to Part II

print that they did not think to invoke the theory in that medium. Whatever the reasons, the writer was allowed more freedom to exhibit human learning than the preacher.

Not all pagans were in the same category; some were more readily accepted than others. The content of quotations was also relevant, but it could be rationalized more easily than an author's reputation. Of all classical authors, the moralists, historians, and philosophers—in roughly that order—met the fewest objections and appeared most frequently in puritan writing. When useful examples or moral precepts could be found among the pagans, the puritans were ready to despoil them and to decorate the temple of Christian didacticism with their riches. Henry Wilkinson shows how widely and generally some of the classical authors were accepted when he cites their popularity—along with that of a few modern writers—as an analogy to his use of sources and a justification of his practice: "If I have fallen in with the conceptions of others, I suppose I shall be no more blamed than they, who writing of poverty, or grief, or death, have made use of Seneca or Plutarch, or they that have handled politics, have consulted with Aristotle's maxims, or have borrowed of Thucydides, and Tacitus, and Polybius, and Philip de Comines, and Lipsius and Guiccardini, who have scattered excellent notions concerning that subject." [13] Though death was a central theme in puritan writings, and a particular attitude toward it distinguished the Christian spirit from the classical, the words of Seneca or Plutarch were perfectly acceptable, in some contexts, to puritans who wrote of it.

Much notice has been given William Walwyn's quotation and praise of Montaigne, but in his time the opponents who held up the practice to his discredit were no more orthodox, and less conventional, than he. Certainly he was unique among the Levellers in professing admiration for secular literature, but if one enlarges the frame of reference to include even the Independents, let alone the puritans as a whole, Walwyn seems unusual chiefly for his relative ignorance of classical literature and thought. His

---

[13]Henry Wilkinson, *Miranda, Stupenda* (1646), sig. A3.

enthusiasm for Thucydides is perfectly traditional, though a bit naive in expression. His use of Montaigne seems merely a compensation for his unfamiliarity with the usual classical authorities. His injunction, "Go to this honest papist or to these innocent cannibals, to learn civility, humanity, simplicity of heart; yea charity and Christianity," [14] is entirely consistent with Hieron's theory that heathens might be used to shame Christians, since in context a papist was as much a religious and moral opponent as a pagan; and Hieron had allowed the practice even in sermons, whereas Walwyn was issuing merely a controversial pamphlet and therefore subject to fewer restrictions.

Analogous comments utilizing classical history and literature are numerous; for example, Whately exclaimed, "O then how just both blame and shame must be cast upon us, that are nothing so regardful of our country's welfare (the most of us) as were some inhabitants of heathen Rome and Athens!" [15] Bolton was no less typical when he found among the heathen "admirable lights of uprightness and honesty" who would, by their example, impugn the faith of many at the Last Judgment: "Cato and Fabricius shall at that day rise up against many lukewarm professors of our times, to their eternal shame, confusion, and condemnation." [16] The use of a man as an example and the use of quotations may appear to be different practices, but in effect they were united under the heading of use of the pagans in Christian religious writings and were admitted or proscribed together in puritan theory.

However useful and admirable the heathen often seemed, their virtues, of course, were only in the realm of natural morality, and saving knowledge could not be gained from them alone. Their virtues might greatly shame Christians in such natural matters as patriotism, but they had been insufficient to save the pagans from damnation. John Goodwin was one of a small

---

[14] William Walwyn, *Walwyns Just Defence* (1649), 11. For a thorough and detailed study of the writings of the Levellers see Joseph Frank, *The Levellers* (Cambridge, Mass.: Harvard University Press, 1955).

[15] Whately, *Charitable Teares* (1623), 192; this edition is bound after *A Care-Cloth* (1624) and *Mortification* (1623), with consecutive pagination.

[16] Robert Bolton, *Discourse About the State of True Happiness*, 18.

and unpopular minority when he suggested that the light of nature, which was all the pagans had been granted, might lead men to knowledge of Christ and so to salvation. [17] But many other puritans, in spite of their dislike of any hint of Pelagianism, admired the pagans enough to be reluctant to stress the fact of their damnation. Sibbes emphasized instead the natural, earthly rewards the pagans had earned: "So far as they exercised the natural goodness that was in them, their consciences reflected peace," and "God gave even them some rewards, upon the discharge of their duties." [18] Other puritans were ready enough to proclaim the ineffectuality of all heathen good works and not concerned to make the stern decrees of God appear just and merciful to human reason, or—as they would have said—to human sentimentality; yet even the most strict believers in the ultimate depravity of all natural gifts frequently praised the very heathens they were sentencing to eternal, hopeless perdition by freely acknowledging the superiority of some heathens to many Christians in the realm of nature. For example, Christopher Love, to emphasize God's mercy to Christians and to evoke humility, gratitude, and puritan optimism, pointed out that "you shall find a holy Cato, a chaste Socrates, a meek Seneca, a just Aristides, these men burn in hell, and thou, an unholy, and unchaste, and impatient, and unjust creature brought to heaven." [19] Greenham paid similarly high tribute to the heathen while he, unlike Sibbes, denied them even a temporal reward, as he pointed out that "even their wise philosophers, sweet orators, and exquisite poets," whose art and virtue were thoroughly commendable, were prone to commit suicide "when once some great distress of mind did wound them." [20]

The phrase, "as the heathen man sayeth," regularly introduced classical quotations, and it appeared frequently, especially before quotations from Seneca and Plutarch, who were the pagan

---

[17] John Goodwin, *The Pagans Debt and Dowry* (1651). Goodwin's premise is that Christ atoned for all men.

[18] Sibbes, *Works*, VII, 355.

[19] Christopher Love, *The Zealous Christian* (1657), 119.

[20] Greenham, *Works*, 149.

authorities most extensively used by the puritans. The qualify
ing phrase apparently reflected no discredit on the value of
the words themselves. Similarly, the phrase, "the heathen man,"
before the names of Cato and Socrates did not make their examples of virtuous living of less force. For the puritans, the most
important theoretical distinction between authorities was not
between Christian and non-Christian writings, for the Fathers
of the Church were treated with much the same caution as the
heathens. The main gulf lay between the Bible and all other
documents and records. However, the Fathers were often so
apposite and useful in controversy, where they proved the antiquity of many interpretations of Scriptures and of many doctrines, that the gulf was often bridged. It was then a relatively
easy passage to the words of the heathen, even the poets. Whereas in theory the Bible was the only authority and all other works
were highly suspect, in practice there was a hierarchy of authorities to be consulted after the Bible, with modern reformed divines in first place, followed by the church Fathers, who were
somewhat tainted by suspicion of heresy, and then at some
distance by the scholastic theologians, who merited respect by
some of their pronouncements on morality. After them came
the heathen moralists, whose word was highly respected in all
questions of natural morality. In last place were the poets, not
absolutely distinguished from the prose moralists, but especially
suspect because as a group they had to their discredit a large
corpus of amoristic works and were thought often to seek elegance of expression at the expense of truth. The categories
overlapped, of course, and Virgil was quoted as respectfully,
though not so boldly, as Seneca. Among the poets a hierarchy of
merit placed the epic poets in first place, followed by the sa-
tirists, with lyric poets well below.

As far down in the scale as the poets were, the road to them
was clear and smooth for many puritan writers, who were able
simultaneously to fix their eyes directly on the Bible and to catch
peripheral glimpses of Virgil, Homer, Horace, or Ovid. For example, Thomas Becon could in one sentence couple examples
of longevity from such diverse sources as pagan legend and the

Old Testament, mentioning "the flourishing years of Nestor, or the long life of Methuselah," and this in a pietistic work. [21] The writer of the preface to Hieron's *Four Learned and Godly Sermons* finds examples for an argument in the Bible and in Virgil, and gives no indication of any difference in authority or validity: "He hath not the smooth voice of Jacob and rough hand of Esau, nor was he like Drances, Turnus his adversary, *Lingua melior sed frigida bello dextera.*" [22] Although both writers were dealing with natural phenomena and did not need to depend on revealed knowledge, the combination of sources is noteworthy because it appears so frequently in puritan writings and because of the puritan view of the uniqueness of the Bible. More surprising, although common, is Arrowsmith's use of a pagan writer to help explain a Biblical text in a religious context. In a controversial work about the covenant, he quotes part of Leviticus 26:24: "Then will I also walk contrary unto you." He explains it first in his own words: "that is, war against you by my judgments, as you have fought against me by your sins"; and then for further explanation he calls upon Ovid: " 'Tis the nature of contraries so to do: *Frigida pugnabant calidis, humentia siccis*, heat and cold, moisture and drought expel each other." [23]

In another appearance in moral and religious works, the heathen poets were featured as opponents who admitted some point, thereby evidencing that it was universally admitted and hence indisputable. Whately, arguing that an idle person will prove an adulterer whereas "the diligent hand, joined with hearty prayer to God, will preserve a man (at least a married man) pure and undefiled," cited the poets who would be the last to express the sentiment if it were disputable: "The most amorous of all the band of amorists (the poets) felt and confessed this to be so." [24] The logical core of the argument is the common formula "If even they admit it, it must be so." A similar and equally popular formula might be stated, "If even the

[21] Thomas Becon, *The Sicke Mans Salve* (1607), sig. A2v.
[22] Hieron, *Works*, preface to Part II, by W. Y.
[23] John Arrowsmith, *The Covenant-Avenging Sword* (1643), 2-3.
[24] Whately, *A Bride-Bush*, 9.

heathen thought so (or did so), surely the Christian must think
so (or do so)." This logic is used by Thomas Goodwin and
Thomas Ball, for example, with a quotation from Horace in the
dedicatory epistle to Preston's *Golden Sceptre*; in praise of the
work they write, "If he could say, *non omnis moriar* because he
was a poet, and think his poem, *perennius aere*, a monument that
time itself would not be able to devour: how much more may
he say it that draws himself unto the life in an immortal dye,
and writes such characters as are not subject to decay and
perish?" [25] A Biblical quotation is used to develop the theme
further. The implied logic may be dubious, but indubitable is
the fact that many puritans so used quotations readily and
without any reservations about the suitability of the practice.

Examples could be multiplied, but a few striking uses of pagan
quotations should be enough to demonstrate the puritans' devotion to classical writers. One would not expect pagan words with
a pagan religious significance to be admissible in Christian religious writings. Yet, to express his horror at the cavaliers' re-
puted contempt for the gospel, Christopher Love used the words
of Virgil's Sybil: *Procul, o procul, este profani.* [26] Nor would one
expect to find one of the most amorous of the poems of the amorists used in a religious argument. Yet, Robert Bolton, in a work
which became a classic of puritan eschatology, used Catullus'
"Vivamus, Mea Lesbia" to warn the Christian reader against plac-
ing too much value on this life, and he cited the poet, though
apologetically, as an authority, not as a negative example. As
if to heighten the paradox, Bolton introduced his quotation with
a quotation from Raleigh's *History of the World*:

> This swift tide of man's life, after it once turneth and de-
> clineth, ever runneth with a perpetual ebb and falling stream,
> but never floweth again: Our leaf once fallen, springeth no
> more; neither do the sun or summer beautify us again with
> the garments of new leaves and flowers, or ever after revive
> or renew us with freshness of youth and former strength. Not
> only Solomon (Eccles. 1) makes us in this respect more

[25]Preston, *The Golden Sceptre* (1638), ep. ded.
[26]Christopher Love, *The Debauched Cavalleer* (1642), 4.

miserable than the sun and other soulless creatures; but even the poet, also by the light of natural reason (whom I urge only to make Christians, mindless of their own mortality, ashamed, who have thoughts of heaven and earth, as though eternity were upon earth, and time only in heaven) tells us that *Soles occidere et redire possunt*: Thus in English:

> The sun may set and rise:
> But we contrariwise,
> Sleep after one short light,
> An everlasting night.

Which we must only understand of returning any more to life and light in this world.

Bolton gives an orthodox reason for the use of pagans in religious works; yet the quotation is not really apposite. He and Catullus have in common the *memento mori* idea, but the *carpe diem* argument of Catullus' poem is diametrically opposite to Bolton's, and in the last line of his translation Bolton runs into an ostensible meaning that he must explain away. [27]

Bolton was apparently not greatly worried that his quotation would evoke the original poem and bring before his readers the tempting notion of making the most of today. And he was by no means alone in his willingness to take the risk. Gataker quoted in the margin of a funeral sermon, opposite a discussion of the uncertainty and brevity of man's life, the original of two of the lines Bolton translated: *Nobis cum semel occidit brevis lux, nox est perpetua una dormienda*, and drew a parallel sentiment from Job. [28] And the same passage occurs in a sermon delivered before Parliament: "Our life is a day, and our death a night, a long night after a short winter's day. If we neglect to work that day, what followeth? *Nox est perpetua, una dormienda*: a dismal and an eternal night." [29] In each instance, the context of the Latin words had to be ignored. Moreover, there was no compelling reason for using the passage; one must sus-

---

[27] Robert Bolton, *Mr. Boltons Last and Learned Worke of the Foure Last Things, Death, Judgement, Hell, and Heaven* (1633), 43-44.

[28] Gataker, *Jeroboams Sonnes Decease* (1627), 12.

[29] Richard Love, *The Watchmans Watchword* (1642), 19. Love's puritan sympathies were not strong, but he was in favor even with puritan extremists.

pect that when the puritans thought of death, the vivid image
of Catullus came to mind, and that they incorporated it into discourses mainly because of the poetic charm of the expression,
ignoring its impropriety. And if this poem of Catullus could
be thus Christianized, even in part, with its belief in the
eternality of death, its flagrant worldliness and exaltation of
sensual pleasure, what poem would be inadmissible?

The last examples do not, of course, represent a general rule.
But they should be a useful corrective to an oversimplified view
of puritan theory which focuses only on the works of Perkins,
who was more rigorous than most in avoiding non-Biblical allusions, or on the sermons of such preachers as Whately and Hieron, addressed to relatively unsophisticated congregations to
whom classical allusions would have been incomprehensible and
confusing. Puritan theory was full of cautions, but it was varied
and flexible enough to allow such men as Gataker and Bolton
to draw upon their learning whenever they found it appropriate
to do so. It is in the context of a widespread use of human literature that we must interpret strictures such as Travers' objection to the preachers who "play rather the orators and philosophers than prophets and interpreters of the holy Scripture," and
"stuff their sermons with divers sentences out of philosophers,
poets, orators, and schoolmen, and of the ancient fathers." [30]
Travers was trying to right the balance, but before, during, and
after his time the practice of quoting poets and orators flourished, and was justified in theory. The very arguments against
it in a not over-subtle manner reveal its wide acceptance, among
the puritans as well as among their opponents. Many of the
puritan ministers thus reveal a fondness for the classics of
literature corresponding to their familiarity with them and the
ingenuity with which they were able to adapt them to the
immediate purposes of their writings.

---

[30] Walter Travers, *A Full and plaine declaration of Ecclesiasticall Disci-
pline out off the word off God* (1574), 104-105.

CHAPTER 6

Poet and Play-Poet

WHATEVER THE COMPLEXITIES, ambiguities, and differences of opinion among the puritans with regard to other literary matters, their condemnation of the stage was unequivocal and almost univocal. Even when they did not condemn plays explicitly or in detail, they used the terms "stage," "stage-play," and "play-poet" in such an uncompromisingly and inescapably derogatory sense that the force of their authority was applied against plays even in their sermons and treatises on quite other subjects. For example, Daniel Dyke, writing of the temptations resisted by Christ, describes latter-day snares of the devil, which lead men "from the church to the alehouse, the stews, and the stage," condemning the stage indirectly and by association, but forcefully. [1] In another typical use of similar words, Edmund Bagshawe, writing of the wild youth of Robert Bolton, gives a concrete account of his sins by noting that "he loved stage-plays, cards and dice, he was a horrible swearer and Sabbath breaker." [2] The public used to such references must have come to think of the stage as synonymous with vice, and of attendance at plays as unimpeachable evidence of a debauched life.

This attitude toward the stage is not, however, an identifying characteristic of puritanism; it was shared, and often stated, by Anglicans. In fact, few churchmen of any persuasion can be found to defend playhouses. In answering Prynne's attack on the stage and defending the right of his courtier friends to see plays, Laud could apparently say no more than that plays were

---

[1] Dyke, *Two Treatises* (1616), 216.
[2] "Life of Mr. Bolton," prefixed to Robert Bolton, *Four Last Things*.

not *"mala per se,"* as he charged Prynne had maintained, but that stripped of their immoral accompaniments they were "things indifferent." [3] On two other levels of Anglo-Catholic religiosity, both Nicholas Ferrar and Giles Fletcher recorded condemnations of playhouses and play-poets that differ in no way from the puritan. [4]

The effect of the puritan attack on the stage is quite definite in the closing of the theatres and the suspension of public dramatic performances in England for eighteen years. The chronology of the attacks on the stage and their relative influence have been studied. The general motives of the controversialists and the grounds and justice of their attacks have also been established. Many of these topics have no bearing on the puritan attitude toward other forms of literature. For instance, the validity of the universal objections to the theatre as a place of social resort and to the social evils incidental to theatrical performances can be passed over. Irrelevant also are the strictures against the wearing of women's clothing by men, which provided the Biblical warrant, so eagerly sought by the puritans in all controversy, for opposition to drama on religious grounds. In any case, this objection was discredited by seventeenth-century puritan scholars long before the appearance of actresses made it inapplicable. But other puritan arguments have implications for all literature and raise the question of the extent to which the attack on the stage was an attack on literature itself, or at least on the artistic principles that the acted play has in common with the written play, or even poem. In fact, we may well ask simply if the attack on the stage was an attack on literature.

One of the puritan objections to plays was identical with the objection to romances and ballads; both competed with religion for the time and attention of the public. The theatre was especially bad because of its analogy with the church as a gathering place, and the implications of many puritan statements are that the common people often went to see plays when they might and should have gone to hear sermons. Northbrooke lamented

---

[3]Cullen, "Puritanism and the Stage," 177.
[4]Holaday, "Giles Fletcher and the Puritans," 579, 585.

that "many can tarry at a vain play two or three hours, whenas they will not abide scarce one hour at a sermon." [5] In a very tangible way the sermon was in competition with a theatrical performance, and the written sermon with a printed play. The discrepancy in moral content, tone, and function between the religious and secular activities made the competition a painful one for the ministers. They strove to exploit the discrepancy in their attacks on the established church, and at the same time to direct it away from themselves, by comparing the Mass with a play and the "mass-priest" with an actor. [6] The analogy probably led to some of the attacks on the use of ostentatious language and histrionic gestures in the pulpit. It is interesting to speculate how often the preacher was conscious that as he tried to impress lessons on his hearers, to preach powerfully, he was using rhetorical and oratorical techniques that invited comparison with those of actors. But whether or not he achieved that painful degree of self-consciousness, the minister did perceive a competition between sermon and play, between preacher and actor, which heightened the vehemence of his attack on the stage. Once underway, the conflict generated its own sustaining impetus. The puritan who was conscious of a serious mission and read or heard of Zeal of the Land Busy on the English stage would become all the more intransigent and sweeping in his condemnation of the plays and of everyone associated with them. [7] For instance, William Crashaw writes in a tone of outrage that the actors "bring religion and holy things upon the stage," and objects specifically to the use of the names of churches to designate hypocrites in a play. [8]

Anger with such representations, and a strongly felt need to deny any similarity between the grave, moral profession of the minister and the frivolous, vicious business of the actor and

---

[5]John Northbrooke, *A Treatise against Dicing, Dancing, Plays, and Interludes with Other Idle Pastimes*, ed. John Payne Collier, from ed. of 1577 (London: Shakespeare Society, 1843), 94.

[6]William Prynne, *Histrio-Mastix* (1633), 935.

[7]For a detailed account of stage caricatures of puritans, especially ministers, see Holden, *Anti-Puritan Satire*, 94-144.

[8]William Crashaw, *The Sermon Preached at the Cross, Feb. xiii. 1607* (1608), 172.

playwright often blinded the puritans to the nature and value of imaginative representation in art. Stubbes, for instance, refused to tolerate the argument that plays might offer "many a good example"; he rejects the very argument advanced by Spenser in support of *The Faerie Queene* and accepted by nearly all Renaissance theorists of literature, including Sidney and Milton. But to Stubbes it was a "blasphemy intolerable" that "filthy plays and bawdy interludes" should be likened in moral efficacy to sermons, "to the word of God." Some of the puritans struck at the basis of art in statements that denied any significance to imitation of reality by treating imitation as lying or by deliberately confusing it with fact. Stubbes's rhetorical question, "Who will call him a wise man, that playeth the part of a fool and vice?" extended by several parallel questions in the same vein, indicates that the acted role is not to be distinguished from everyday life in applying moral judgments. [9] It would deny to art the representation of evil, for evil represented is treated as an occurrence of sin.

Conversely, a critic of the stage might object to the discrepancy between the actor and his role, and so would reject as a lie the character in a drama. For instance, Robert Bolton, discussing hypocrisy, traces the word to the Greek name for an actor: "it signified a stage-player, who sometimes putteth on the robes and majesty of a prince, himself being of a base and neglected state; or the gravity and wisdom of a counselor, himself being of roguish and dissolute conditions." [10] Bolton, whose works sparkle with classical allusions, did not attack the stage directly, though like nearly all puritans, he made numerous derogatory references to it in his work. However, this indirect reference is significant because it arises from a refusal to accept dramatic conventions and thus embodies a basic, though not explicit, at-

[9] *Philip Stubbes's Anatomy of the Abuses in England in Shakspere's Youth A. D. 1583*, ed. Frederick J. Furnivall (London: The New Shakspere Society, 1877), 143-46. In a preface to the early editions, Stubbes admitted some plays were "honest and commendable," but the omission of the preface from the editions of 1585 and 1595 probably constitutes a withdrawal of this concession.

[10] Robert Bolton. *Discourse About the State of True Happiness*, 30.

tack on all forms of art, including poetry. Like Bacon's slighting reference to poetry as "the shadow of a lie," it at least disparages whatever it permits.

The denial of the validity of imitation and imaginative representation of reality was an attitude rather than a belief with many of those who expressed it, and it appears only in occasional references. Stubbes, for instance, used it when it served his argument but did not adhere to it consistently. Few puritans ever examined the question theoretically, and Baxter, by doing so, made a valuable contribution to understanding of the attack on the stage. Generally in his writings, Baxter merely rehearses the usual objections against the social evils of the theatre; but in resolving a case of conscience he addresses himself to the question "whether stage-plays where the virtuous and vicious are personated are lawful?" [11] He develops his answer methodically, following the characteristic puritan method of stating a liberal general principle and then gradually restricting it by progressively more severe qualifications and exceptions. From Christ's parables, featuring persons with no existence in actual history, Baxter derives the principle that "it is not absolutely unlawful to personate another man." As a logical corollary to this axiom, "to personate good men in good actions is not simply unlawful." Like Sidney and other defenders of poetry, Baxter makes the important distinction between imitation and falsehood: "personating" is not lying because "it is not an asserting . . . nor so taken." The acceptance of mimetic art is clear enough, though the existence of the question answered by Baxter indicates that the opposite view had gained some influence.

In approving the representation of good men and actions, Baxter narrowed his question to the moral content of drama and came, by a more devious path, to nearly the same practical conclusions as those who saw the evil on the stage as real evil. His statement, "To personate a bad man in a bad action is more dubious, but seemeth not to be in all cases unlawful," betrays, in its emphasis, a strong hesitation to approve plays. To be lawful, evil actions and persons must be presented, as they seldom

---

[11] Baxter, *Christian Directory*, 877.

are, with the "shame and hatred and grief which should rightly affect the hearers with an abhorrence of them." The dominant moral concern of the puritans determines the conditions. The criterion is the ultimate moral effect of the representation upon the audience, and the audience reaction is assumed to correspond with the attitude of the artist and the tone of his work.

On the treatment of evil, Baxter does not cite the relevant Biblical text, but one can find it in many puritan attacks on the stage. Perkins, for instance, quotes and interprets it: "St. Paul saith fornication, and covetousness, let them not be named amongst you, as becometh Saints, *Eph.* 5:3. And if vices of men may not be named, unless the naming of them, tend to the reproving and further condemning of them, much less may they be represented for the causing of mirth and pleasure." [12] Perkins' exception was necessary if the preachers were to take up questions of morality, and it was justified by the practice of the apostles. Baxter simply made a further explicit exception for representations—an exception not entirely inconsistent with Perkins' statement, which merely condemned representation of vice for "mirth and pleasure." Since in Baxter's theory the parables justified stage representations, discussions of evil in sermons might, by a further development of the same reasoning, justify its representation on the stage. And it is characteristic of the puritans that, however often they might quote St Paul, they did not feel that the mere naming or description of vice would harm the audience, if it were combined with the proper instructions. In general, their belief in the efficacy of instruction was stronger, or at least nearer the surface of their consciousness, than their belief in human depravity.

From his theory of representations, Baxter concludes logically, "I think it possible to devise and act a comedy or tragedy, which should be lawful, and very edifying. It might be so ordered by wise men." But in his very next sentences he retreats from this liberal position: "I think I never knew or heard of a lawful stage-play, comedy, or tragedy in the age that I have lived in." And subsequently he details fifteen objections against the the-

---

[12] Perkins, *The Whole Treatise of the Cases of Conscience* (1651), 314.

atre and plays of his day: (1) they represent vices "viciously" and needlessly; (2) they use words which are materially false, and so corrupt speech; (3) they use vain words; (4) they employ amorous expressions; (5) they consume precious time; (6) they take the place of more honest recreation; (7) they appeal to the most sensual people; (8) they are repugnant to the "best and wisest persons"; (9) they are expensive; (10) they rival the church, as if they were the devil's temples; (11) the players make a trade of mere recreation; (12) plays are not associated with godly persons in Scripture; (13) primitive Christians and churches condemned plays; (14) they have harmed "thousands of young people"; and (15) at best "they are controverted and of doubtful lawfulness." [13] Thus Baxter ultimately denies in practice what he grants in theory, as so many puritans did on so many occasions. For the English stage the difference between his theory and one that rejected drama in principle is merely academic; but for poetry and the other arts, the difference is significant. The mimetic arts have been sanctioned, and poetry and prose fiction can be judged on their merits.

Restrictions, like Baxter's, on the representation of vice were inevitably extended to other forms of literature. In the work of some of the opponents of the stage they were stressed so emphatically that the result seemed a denial of poetry. In fact, a tension between liberal general principles and restrictive specifications was common in the puritan attitude toward poetry, but the general principles were more readily stated and the specific objections less emphatic and more equivocal than in puritan statements on drama. Among the leading writers in the stage controversy, among the classics of the puritans' literary campaign against the theatre, the earliest writer, Northbrooke, did not bring poetry into question. Northbrooke attacked the theatre primarily as a social institution, as a place and means of recreation. He not only accepted drama in theory, but unlike many others, he approved, with restrictions, the acting of plays in the schools. The restrictions are numerous and typical: school plays should not contain "ribaudry or filthy terms"; they

---

[13]Baxter, *Christian Directory*, 877-78.

should be performed in Latin, as Latin exercises; they should be infrequent; they should not employ lavish costumes; they should not be acted for profit; and they should not use amorous themes. Only the last restriction has clear implications for poetry; like other puritans, Northbrooke would condemn the love lyric. [14]

In the more forceful and truculent argument of Stubbes, literature does not fare so well. Whatever his theory, the tone of his argument is such that little but explicitly religious and moral writing seems acceptable. Stubbes, in fact, has reservations about music, which he approves only when used for a religious purpose or "privately in a man's secret chamber or house." He condemns "wicked books . . . profane schedules, sacrilegious libels, and ethnical pamphlets of toys and bobleries" and laments the unpopularity of any "godly treatise, reproving vice and teaching virtue." The kind of reading approved by Stubbes may be inferred from his praise of Fox's "worthy book of martyrs." [15]

The comments of Stubbes and Northbrooke are less significant by themselves than when placed next to Gosson's, for Gosson's work makes explicit many attitudes and principles which the others merely suggest. Because he answered the objections raised against his attack on the stage, Gosson had occasion to state some principles that the others could pass by. For instance, in his *Apology* for *The School of Abuse*, he tries to deny many implications that others saw in the earlier work. In his words, "they that are grieved are poets, pipers, players; the first think that I banish poetry, wherein they dream; the second judge that I condemn music, wherein they dote; the last proclaim that I forbid recreation to man, wherein you may see they are stark blind." [16] The acceptance of poetry, music, and recreation in principle is asserted unequivocally. But taking the poets only—though the pipers and players could make a similar argument—one can find a potent stimulus for their dreams. In the *School of Abuse* Gosson treats their work with scant respect, having found in it

---

[14]Northbrooke, *Treatise*, 104.
[15]Stubbes, *Anatomy of Abuses*, 171, 185.
[16]Stephen Gosson, *A Short Apologie of the Schoole of Abuse (1579)*, ed. Edward Arber (London: English Reprints, 1868), 65.

little of that all-important moral content which he thought the sole justification of writing. He cites with approval the comment on poets in the *Republic* which distressed many Renaissance apologists for literature, including Sidney: "No marvel though Plato shut them out of his school, and banished them quite from his commonwealth, as effeminate writers, unprofitable members, and utter enemies to virtue." Even their moral precepts are suspect or defective: "Many good sentences . . . are written by poets as ornaments to beautify their works, and set their trumpery to sale without suspect." [17] Skeptical of attempts to Christianize, or even moralize, pagan works through allegorical interpretation, he writes scornfully of "wresting the rashness of Ajax, to valor; the cowardice of Ulysses, to policy; the dotage of Nestor, to grave counsel; and the battle of Troy to the wonderful conflict of the four elements; where Juno, which is counted the air, sets in her foot to take up the strife, and steps boldly betwixt them to part the fray." [18] The only specific value he allows to poetry he limits to the classics: "The right use of ancient poetry was to have the notable exploits of worthy captains, the wholesome councils of good fathers, and the virtuous lives of predecessors set down in numbers and sung to the instrument at solemn feasts, that the sound of the one might draw the hearers from kissing the cup too often; the sense of the others put them in mind of things past, and chalk out the way to do the like." [19] Moreover Gosson's phrases practically echo Webbe, who calls the Homeric epic the "truest, ancientest, and best kind of poetry" after describing what moral philosophy and practical statecraft can be learned from Homer. [20] Apposite also are Sidney, and Spenser's letter to Raleigh. But unlike the apologists, Gosson proceeds to fence in ancient poetry, to build a wall between it and the modern. Moreover, he has already written scornfully of the ancient

[17]Gosson, *The Schoole of Abuse (1579)*, ed. Edward Arber (London: English Reprints, 1868) , 20.

[18]*Ibid.,* 21.

[19]*Ibid.,* 25. Sidney's praise of the inspirational effect of the popular ballad of Percy and Douglas may well be a direct reference to this passage, an attempt to show that valor can be aroused by modern poems also.

[20]William Webbe, "A Discourse of English Poetrie," in Smith, ed., *Elizabethan Critical Essays,* I, 235.

epic, and in the *Apology* he quotes Cicero as the authority for a denunciation of "ancient poets" as the "fathers of lies, pipes of vanity, and schools of abuse," mainly because they ascribed immorality to the gods. [21] The right use of poetry seems to have been its employment among the Greeks to gain immediate, practical, moral ends, and to have little significance for Gosson's own time. Doubtless Gosson did feel that he was not attacking poetry as an art; but once involved in controversy, he found arguments against it easier to set down than to qualify.

Gosson and most of the other controversialists apparently saw no great distinction between the printed and the acted play; the term "play-book" was as derogatory as the term "stage-play." But they were seldom pressed for a distinction. Rainolds, however, had to refine his arguments because he was engaged in a debate, and his distinctions are interesting. Although his condemnation of plays was sweeping, and he made no exceptions for drama acted in schools, he nevertheless admitted that a play might be read, in private or before an audience, without harm. His example suggests that other controversialists, who were otherwise no more strict than he, might likewise have made the allowance had they been provoked or compelled to do so. Rainolds, answering William Gager, declares first of all that he does not "despise learned poetry." Basing his argument on the familiar example of St. Paul, he quotes Tertullian's remark that "St. Paul hath sanctified a verse of Menander." Logically, if some of Menander is sanctified but the theatre is condemned, the reading of plays is permitted. Rainolds takes the lawfulness of reading poetry as an implied axiom, not explicitly allowing it, but using it to justify the reading of plays. Answering another question, he grants that Seneca may be recited, and declares that he has recited Seneca in the classroom. For the distinction that permits reciting and condemns acting, he cites as authorities Pliny, Juvenal, and Scaliger; reciting is no more a loss of time and no more dangerous to morality than reading. Thus Rainolds draws a clear line between the proper and improper use

---

[21]Gosson, *Apology*, 65-66.

of plays; and the reading of both plays and poetry is well on the safe side of it. [22]

How many other puritans made a similar distinction is not clear. But a substantial number, because of Rainolds' authority alone, probably did not think of the plays of Seneca or Menander when they wrote against the stage, and even against playbooks. The primary objection was to the social institution. The more rigorous of them were not so much uncompromising as they were undiscriminating. They aimed their blows at theatres and actors, and if some quite moral and venerable tragedy came within the range by entering the public or private theatre, it too became their victim, as might any poet who happened along when they were in a truculent mood. But if the play or poem came to the study respectably labelled and insisting upon being treated on its merits, they were ready to apply the criterion of moral efficacy and to praise or blame accordingly.

It was the moral tendency rather than the moral content alone that determined acceptability. As Baxter said, vice might be represented if accompanied by expressions of hatred or disgust. Amorous themes were generally proscribed, but perhaps because they were never handled with the proper cautions. The ordinance of 1642, which closed the theatres, is clear enough in its emphasis on the tone and quality of moral attitude. It noted that plays as "spectacles too commonly expressing lascivious mirth and levity" were ill-suited to the sad times. Doubtless the objection to levity has strengthened the concept of glum, ascetic puritanism. But as we have seen, and as the ordinance specifies, levity was objectionable when it was derived from portrayal of vice, not on every occasion; the time, place, and effect determine the suitability of the attitude. After all, part of John Dod's great reputation was based on his wit and humor.

The best summary of puritan opinion concerning drama is the monumental attack on the stage by William Prynne. Generally regarded as an extremist, both by his contemporaries and later readers, Prynne gained his unpleasant reputation not so

[22]Rainolds, *Overthrow of Stage-Plays*, 21-22.

much from the substance of his argument as by his contentious manner of expression and his unfortunate, probably uninten-tional, insult to the queen. Except for topical allusions, Prynne's discursive and prolix volume offers nothing original; it is largely a compilation of material from sources best described by his title page: "of sundry texts of Scripture; of the whole primitive church, both under the law and gospel; of 55 synods and coun-cils; of 71 Fathers and Christian writers, before the year of our Lord, 1200; of above 150 foreign and domestic Protestant and Popish authors, since; of 40 heathen philosophers, historians, poets; of many heathen, many Christian nations, republics, em-perors, princes, magistrates; of sundry apostolical, canonical, im-perial constitutions; and of our own English statutes, magistrates, universities, writers, preachers." Prynne quoted extensively and thereby gave his work one significant merit: it is an encyclo-paedia of attacks, incorporating practically all the English writ-ings on the subject before his time.

Prynne's main thesis, also stated on the title page, highlights the chief basis of the puritan attack. He is writing to prove "that popular stage-plays . . . are sinful, heathenish, lewd, un-godly spectacles, and most pernicious corruptions, condemned in all ages, as intolerable mischiefs to churches, to republics, to the manners, minds, and souls of men. And that the profession of play-poets, of stage-players; together with the penning, acting, and frequenting of stage plays, are unlawful, infamous, and mis-beseeming Christians." Noteworthy here is the emphasis on the theatre as a social institution, and on the social effects of the acted play. The repetition of the word "stage," especially when it qualifies the attack on play-poets, also limits the scope of the attack. Drama as an art form is outside the field of inquiry as Prynne defined it. In fact, with a curious propriety, he sub-divided the vast book into acts and scenes instead of the conven-tional books and chapters, thus giving approval to use of at least the superficialities of dramatic form.

In cursory statements Prynne often seemed to reject all litera-ture except the Bible and religious works arising from it. Like other puritans, he saw a competition between secular writings and religious. The reading of plays, compared with the reading of the Bible and other religious works, is a dangerous waste of time. [23] It is an active, present danger because "above forty thousand playbooks" have been "printed within these two years" and are "now more vendible than the choicest sermons." [24] In addition to playbooks, Prynne condemns "the ordinary reading of comedies, tragedies, Arcadias, amorous histories, poems and other profane discourses." Traditionally, he cites the dream of St. Jerome, with its implied rejection of "Ciceronian" or classical learning and literature. [25] Encountering the text of Matthew 12:36: "But I say unto you, that every idle word that men shall speak, they shall give account thereof in the day of judgment," he finds himself unable to justify any writing that does not work directly for salvation. From these comments one could infer that Prynne was a single-minded fanatic, and could extend the inference to the puritans as a whole, for the attitudes are typical. But in context, Prynne, like many others, was trying to right a balance; he was striking at the center of his opponents' position, not with the intention of destroying it, but with the hope of bypassing and rendering indefensible the outlying positions which seemed to infringe on the territory of religion and piety.

His argument is much more temperate when he develops his attitude toward poetry logically. But by defending poetry, he acknowledges that his argument against plays could be applied by his readers to more than the stage. He seeks to limit his attack by acknowledging that "poetry itself is an excellent endowment . . . useful and commendable among Christians, if rightly used." Inevitably, he cites Paul's three quotations which "canonized" heathen literature. Unlike most puritans, he gives a list of approved poets, including both Christian and classical: "not only the divine hymns recorded in Scripture together with the famous ancient poems of Tertullian, Arator, Apollinaris, Nazianzen, Prudentius, Prosper, and other Christian worthies, with the modern distichs of Du Bartas, Beza, Scaliger, Bucanon, Heinsius, Withars, Alley, Quarles, our late sovereign King James,

[23]Prynne, *Histriomastix*, 307.
[24]*Ibid.*, ep. ded.
[25]*Ibid.*, 923-25.

with infinite others; but likewise the much applauded verses of
Homer, Pindarus, Virgil, Statius, Silius Italicus, Lucan, Claudian,
Horace, Juvenal, and some parts of Ovid, where he is not obscene." [26] These authors he approves for general reading and for
use in the schools. The mingling of classical and Christian writings, and the fact that Prynne makes the list representative. not
exclusive, give a humanistic tone to his discussion.

The qualified approval of Ovid and subsequent exclusion of
several classical writers somewhat darken the aspect of Prynne's
humanism, but do not quite obscure it. As he sanctions poets who
might have a formative effect, he rejects those he considers irreligious, frivolous, or amorous. Using the traditional argument
of the censor, he condemns not only what is bad in itself, but
what might tend to corrupt women and youths; and he draws a
clear distinction between the two considerations. For instance,
he mentions with approval a law of the Jews forbidding those
under thirty years of age to read Canticles; although the morality
of the work is unimpeachable, the young may "draw those spiritual love passages to a carnal sense, and make them instruments
to inflame their lusts." [27] Puritanical as this attitude may sound,
it is to be found frequently enough outside puritan writing.
Even the opponent of Martin Marprelate, Thomas Nashe, who
had enough difficulties with censors to be wary of them, urges
censorship of books for youth. After mentioning Ovid's obscen-
ity, Nashe argues that "tender youth ought to be restrained for
a time from the reading of such ribaldry, lest chewing over
wantonly the ears of this summer corn, they be choked with the
haun before they can come at the kernel." [28]

In the literature of his time, Prynne denounces, characteristically, "the reading of lascivious, amorous, scurrilous playbooks,
histories, and Arcadias," again largely out of concern for "women
and youths." The medieval romance gets harsh treatment in
Prynne's one example, the *Romaunt of the Rose*, against which
he quotes denunciation of both the work and its authors. On

---

[26]*Ibid.*, 832.
[27]*Ibid.*, 914-21.
[28]Thomas Nashe, "The Anatomie of Absurditie," in Smith, ed., *Elizabethan
Critical Essays*, I, 332.

classical literature, he quotes several English churchmen against "Ovid's wanton epistles and books of love, Catullus, Tibullus, Propertius, Martial, the comedies of Plautus, Terence, and other such amorous books, savoring either of pagan gods, of ethnic rites and ceremonies, or of scurrility, amorousness, and profaneness. [29]

The listing of Plautus and Terence along with the poets is one evidence that Prynne, like Renaissance critics in general, often used *poetry* to mean all imaginative literature. When he does make a clear distinction between the dramatic form and other genres, he nevertheless applies the same criterion of moral efficacy to all kinds of poetry. "It is lawful," he grants, "to compile a poem in nature of a tragedy, or poetical dialogue, to add life and luster to it, especially in case of necessity, whenas truth should else be suffocated." As an example of lawful dramatic writing Prynne exhibits Apollinaris the Elder, who, when forbidden to preach, "translated divers books of Scriptures into verse, and composed divers tragedies in imitation of Euripides, and sundry comedies and lyric verses in imitation of Menander and Pindarus, consisting only of divine arguments and scripture stories." Gregory Nazianzen provides another model. The examples are quite restrictive, but Prynne liberalizes his theory by extending his approval to "the tragedies, comedies, and playpoems of ancient times, such as those of Sophocles, Euripides, Aeschylus, Menander, Seneca, and many others." [30] All of these, Prynne argues, were originally recited or read, not acted. Aristophanes is here passed over in silence, but that he belongs in the restricted category with Terence and Plautus is evident from another mention of him as a "scurrilous, carping comedian" who "traduced and abused virtuous Socrates on the stage." [31] Among the moral English dramatists Prynne lists "John Bale his comedies de Christo and de Lazare, Skelton's comedies de Virtute, de magnificentia, and de bono Ordine, Nicholas Grimaldus de Archiprophetae Tragedia, etc." Again neglecting to distinguish

---

[29]Prynne, *Histriomastix*, 916, 922.
[30]*Ibid.*, 832-34.
[31]*Ibid.*, 121.

genres, he adds "Geffrey Chaucers and Pierce the Plowmans Tales and Dialogues." [32]

The list of classics is impressive, in the face of Prynne's total rejection of the stage. But he apparently believed that the dramatic works, both ancient and modern, that he approved were never intended to be acted; and granting moral content and influence, acting made all the difference. Many plays might lawfully be read, because reading, unlike acting, could be attended to without loss of money or time, without exposure to the bad company of the theatre, and finally "without using or beholding any effeminate, amorous, lustful gestures, compliments, kisses, dalliances, or embracements; any whorish immodest, fantastic womanish apparrel, vizards, disguises; any lively representations of venery, whoredom, adultery and the like, which are apt to enrage men's lusts; without hypocrisy, feigning cheats, lascivious tunes and dances." [33] The distinction between reading and seeing a play is implied in Prynne's summary and qualification of his attack on the play-poet; the point at issue is "not whether it be unlawful to pen a poem in nature of a tragedy or comedy, which may be done without offense if it be pious, serious, good, and profitable; not wanton, obscene, profane, or heathenish, as most plays are now; but whether the profession of a playhouse poet, or the penning of plays for public or private theatres, be warrantable or lawful." [34] The answer was, of course, "no"; but it was applied universally only to the "playhouse," the theatre.

Prynne's comments are especially valuable because most of the other attacks on the stage were sparing of examples. With his characteristic self-assurance and prolixity he did not hesitate to multiply the names of the works he approved and condemned. *Histriomastix* proves that an unequivocal condemnation of the theatre could include an approval not only of many poets, but of classical tragedy and much other drama. It is not a radical conjecture that Prynne was documenting the entire puritan attack on the stage in addition to summarizing it. If so, the im-

---

[32] *Ibid.*, 834.
[33] *Ibid.*, 929-30.
[34] *Ibid.*, 835.

plications for literature are clear enough. Poems, even plays, were acceptable in the study and the classroom if their content was not immoral in its effect on the audience. In other words, even dramatic literature was accepted when it served at least indirectly as a handmaid to divinity in teaching languages or precepts and examples of natural morality; but it was rejected when it tended to encourage immorality or, regardless of its moral quality, when it ascended the stage and began to vie with the preacher for the time and attention of the public, to draw people away from sermons to the bad company of the theatre.

Chapter 7

Poetry as Recreation

THE LITERATURE REJECTED by the puritans can be classified under two large headings: the "immoral" and the "popular." About the first, not much more can usefully be said. The term is vague, and so was its application. Generally it included the libidinous and blasphemous, but acceptance or rejection of anything else depended on the individual censor, and upon the audience and context, for Prynne had reservations about the Song of Solomon while some preachers were able to make use of Catullus, properly excerpted and interpreted. Anyone wishing to distinguish the puritans by means of their applications of moral standards can readily find passages to support a charge of inhuman strictures; but, conversely, one can find evidence of a broad and tolerant view. In truth, the puritans adhered to the moral standards of their day. To distinguish them from their contemporaries of similar education and social position one can say little more than that they insisted somewhat more emphatically that moral criteria be applied to literature.

In rejecting the love lyric under the heading of amorous, wanton verse, the puritans struck at much that we value in the literature of their time, but they did not thereby distinguish themselves from their contemporaries. Ultimately, and ironically, the lyric ran afoul of the same pragmatism that caused humanist and puritan alike to treasure the classics and to approach them with an often narrow didacticism. Both thought literature, including poetry, of value when it furthered civic virtue, military prowess, or respect for religion. Vives would have agreed with Gosson on the "right use of ancient poetry," and when the puritans quoted him they in fact recognized a kinship. The movements diverged only when the puritans placed greater emphasis on the salvation of the soul, but in this emphasis they merely reflected their professional interests and social position as spiritual leaders of largely middle and lower class congregations. Insofar as both were educational reformers, humanist and puritan alike saw nothing but obstacles in the potent and distracting appeal of the love lyric.

The second category of proscribed works is, however, even more often cited or else implicit in discussions of the puritan spirit. The term "popular" was a common denominator applicable to the theatre and to the romances and ballads that the puritans disliked. Of course, the categories overlapped, but the test of popularity with the masses was applied even more often than the moral criterion. The puritans could accept the Homeric and Virgilian heroes, but not Robin Hood; the morality of the former could be and was rationalized while the latter was never seriously examined. The imaginative literature that appealed to the more vulgar of the public, those for whom the preachers developed their plain style and their methodical, practical sermons, was condemned because of the fact of the appeal. The reason can be stated generally as a feeling that such reading was a waste of time which had better be given to sermons, edifying works, and religious exercises. The better its artistry, the greater its appeal was to draw men away from more important business, and hence the more dangerous it became.

The puritan attitude here seems rigorous because it seems to deny the use of literature as recreation. The truth is that the plays, ballads, and romances were looked upon by the puritans as a form of recreation, and placed under the same laws as games or athletic exercises. Were, then, all pastimes condemned, and was one to spend all his time, apart from the activities devoted to earning his subsistence, on religious exercises? The answer is to be found in a highly developed—though not entirely consistent—theory of recreations, which in turn was deduced from the theory of callings. The theory which regulated the occupations, the vocations and avocations of men, does much to explain the attack on the stage, the rejection of popular literature, and the development of the concept of the ascetic puritan.

Not all puritans had the same notion of "callings," but their notions were sufficiently homogeneous that William Perkins' *Treatise of the Vocations* can be called typical as well as influential. The crucial Biblical text was I Corinthians 7:20: "Let every man abide in the same calling wherein he was called." In Perkins' definition, "A vocation or calling is a certain kind of life, ordained and imposed on man by God for the common good." This indeed seems like a general comment on the human condition, of little use to practical divinity, but Perkins subdivided and gave rules. First of all he distinguished a "general calling, the calling of Christianity," imposed on all Christians. Then, each man has a particular calling, or vocation, such as that of a magistrate, minister, master, servant, father, child. One person can fit into several particular categories; his calling is not so much a classifiable occupation as a particular role in society, and Perkins' main concern was to emphasize the need for a particular calling, a definite "state and condition of life in the family, in the Commonwealth, or in the Church." The same emphasis governs his first rule: "Every person of every degree, state, sex, or condition, without exception must have some personal and particular calling to walk in." His second rule is concerned with social unrest: "Every man must judge that particular calling, in which God hath placed him, to be the best calling for him." Then follow three rules which relate the particular calling to the general: "Every man must join the practice of his personal calling with the practice of the general calling of Christianity"; "Such as have public callings must first reform themselves in private"; and "A particular calling must give place to a general calling of a Christian." [1]

One may ask if anyone can avoid having a calling, if the theory is not merely descriptive, in spite of its attempt to give prescriptions. But Perkins believes that any "wandering or straggling persons" and any monk and friar have violated his rules. Essentially the concept of a particular calling seems designed to

[1]Perkins, *Works*, 903, 906-12, preface to *Treatise of the Vocations*.

enforce a feeling of moral responsibility, to encourage social stability, to maintain an institutionalized society, and to discourage vagabondage and adventurism in economics or politics. The general calling, with the precedence granted it, establishes the supremacy of the Christian ethic in all business concerns and activities. In other words, the theory of callings is a program for a stable order in church, family, and state, and an argument that Christianity must permeate and regulate secular institutions.

When the particular calling was in the realm of business or trade, the puritan was sometimes vulnerable to a charge of materialism. Perkins' theory, with its emphasis on religious concerns, would have avoided any subordination of religious to secular business, but as time passed others showed readiness to qualify it. Christopher Love admonished "young converts who will be every day fasting and every day hearing, and in the meantime neglect their outward and necessary callings in the world." Arguing that "God did never so order Religion that it should be a disadvantage to our particular callings in the world," he asked for a balance between work and religious exercises. But although he went on to qualify his argument: "I speak not this to make men worldly, that they should glut themselves with worldly business," [2] his emphasis may have led some to consider their worldly business a divinely prescribed and hence religious exercise and to concentrate on it wholly.

Apart from the particular and general callings, all activity would logically be considered recreation. Among the puritans, emphases on the importance of recreation vary, but a general belief was that recreations should be chosen to aid men in their callings, either by providing a necessary rest of mind or body, or by helping develop physical and mental skills useful in one's

---

[2]Christopher Love, *The Combate between the Flesh and the Spirit* (1654), 52-53. The economic implications of the theory of callings were pointed out by Max Weber; see *The Protestant Ethic and the Spirit of Capitalism*, trans. Talcott Parsons (London: George Allen and Unwin Ltd., 1930), 79-92, *et passim*. Weber's thesis was restated by R. H. Tawney in *Religion and the Rise of Capitalism* (New York: Harcourt, Brace and Company, 1926), 240-46. Valuable supplementary information is given in R. I. Michaelson, "Changes in the Puritan Concept of Calling or Vocation," *New England Quarterly*, XXVI (1953), 315-36.

calling. Generally proscribed were all recreations that in themselves were immoral or impious, or that had no relevance to the calling. Specific regulations are abundant in puritan writings. Perkins, taking up the question "whether recreation be lawful for a Christian man," answers with an emphatic "yes." Recreation provides the body needed rest, and is consistent with Christian liberty. But for Perkins and other puritans, the crucial question follows immediately: "What kinds of recreation and sports are lawful and convenient?" Perkins, typically enough, rejects plays, bear-baiting, cockfighting, and all games of hazard. Cards are of uncertain value; they involve skill and so exercise the mind, but the element of chance makes them highly suspect. As a guide to the choice of lawful recreations Perkins sets up four "rules" or principles: (1) recreations must be "of the best report"; (2) they "must be profitable to ourselves and others, and they must tend also to the glory of God"; (3) their purpose "must be to refresh our bodies and minds"; and (4) their use "must be moderate and sparing" of time and "affections," for "we may not set our hearts upon sports." [3]

Other puritan comments on the subject agree generally with Perkins', though with some differences in emphasis. Hieron apparently permits more freedom in choice and use. Like Perkins he approves sports that are "of good report." He rejects games of hazard and sports "which beget lightness and impudency." But one gets the impression that he would be more lenient than Perkins in resolving a case of conscience, for his belief that sports are lawful is grounded on the text "there is . . . a time to laugh" (Ecclesiastes 3:4). By implication sports are good in themselves, apart from their use in furthering the performance of one's calling. Hieron says less of the utility of sports and puts more stress on the element of Christian liberty. [4] Baxter, on the other hand, drew more rigorous conclusions from principles identical to those of Perkins. At least, by making the lawfulness of recreation more dependent on one's calling, he excluded more. For in-

---

[3]Perkins, *Cases of Conscience*, 342-48. The morality of games of chance was extensively debated in the early seventeenth century. With few exceptions, the puritans refused to condone them.

[4]Hieron, *Works*, 677.

stance, if an activity "have no aptitude to fit us for God's service in our ordinary callings and duty, it can be to us no lawful recreation." [5] Hence, he forbids "pastimes" utterly; the word is an "infamous name," with its connotations of "time wasting," of idle employment of time that might be spent in furthering the work of one's calling. [6] The same consideration dictates Taylor's rigorous statement that "recreation is God's ordinance for the necessary refreshing of the mind or body, or both, and the fitting of either or both to the calling." [7] The differences of opinion, or emphasis, seem to be grounded on the closeness of the relationship demanded between calling and recreation. The more liberal theorists were satisfied with a general relationship, and permitted almost any exercise of body or mind, whereas the more rigorous demanded a specific, concrete relationship.

The question of time, stressed by Baxter, made the puritan theory of sports further restrictive. Almost universally the puritans condemned participation in any kind of sports or recreations on the Lord's Day. At other times the watchword was "moderation," and was left vague and general. Whately, however, made it specific by drawing up two rules prescribing the amount of time to be spent on recreation. First, "recreation must follow labor"; or if it precedes, it must be slight, merely adequate "to fit one for labor," and it should be "as the mower's whetstone or rifle is to his scythe, to sharpen it when it grows dull." Secondly, Whately gives a "general and firm direction" that "it is not lawful for a man in an ordinary course to spend more time in any pastime, upon any day, than in religious exercises. . . . It is utterly unlawful to bestow a larger time any day upon the most lawful delight than in private religious exercises, or at least in a customable course so to do." [8] Between the lines one can discern the omnipresent puritan feeling that all sports are to some degree competitive with religion. The calling had been reconciled with religion, and labor in it was almost sancti-

[5]Baxter, *Christian Directory*, 461.
[6]*Ibid.*, 291.
[7]Taylor, *Works*, 141.
[8]Whately, *The Redemption of Time* (1619), 12.

fied; but sports, even when serviceable to one's particular calling, yet seemed to compete with the practice of one's general
calling, specifically with the hearing of sermons and the reading
of godly, moral treatises.

On the sports to be permitted in the allotted time to carry
out the approved functions, the puritans achieved a surprising
unanimity. They condemned stage plays and dancing as occasions
of sin. They found games of chance intolerable because in them
God was invoked to decide profane matters. They thought idle-
ness merely another opportunity for the devil to use the mind as
his workshop. And they saw only paganism, inconsistent with
the general calling of a Christian, in the May games and other
ceremonies that had a pagan origin. On the other hand, they
allowed in general the traditional sports of the nobility, athlet-
ics, and games of skill. Hunting, archery, fencing developed skills
useful to the nation in wartime. Chess, riddles, and similar
games exercised the wits and stimulated the mind. None of these
lawful sports encouraged social gatherings which might lead to
vicious intercourse. Thus far the puritans seem ascetic, especially because none of the generally approved sports could be
indulged in slothfully or for sensual pleasure alone.

But the asceticism is strongly tempered, if not entirely dis-
solved, by the puritan approval of music. Here was a recreation
that did not fit the criteria; it developed neither the mind nor
the body, nor did it have a specific relationship to any calling.
It thus occupies a unique position in the puritan theory of
recreations. With the exception of several cautions against "idle
songs" and some debate over the lawfulness of its use in churches
—which was another, different question—it met with widespread
approval. Puritans must have been aware that, in their scheme
of callings and recreations, music could be no better than a
pastime, but they nevertheless accepted it without any rigorously
conscientious attempt to justify it. The vague term *solace*,
which could have been, but was not, applied to the psychological
effect of the reading of romances, was very commonly adduced
as the beneficial and unquestionably justifying effect of music
upon the mind and emotions. Whately's comment is typical, "It

is a very good and lawful thing to solace oneself with music and a warrantable recreation, so that it be not abused." [9] *Abuse* may here be defined as too frequent or too-long-sustained use; the puritans had surprisingly little to say about the possibly corrupting effects of "soft Lydian airs." In their appreciation of music, many puritans unabashedly used an art for the pleasure that it gave them, without troubling to justify it by moral or strictly practical considerations.

Inevitably one must ask why, of all the arts, music was singled out for widespread approval. Why, for instance, was not poetry also praised as a recreation with which one might solace himself? Paradoxically, the puritan's high esteem for music, his usual exemption of it from the criticism and suspicions directed at the other arts, arose from its nonrepresentational nature, which severely restricted not only its power for good, but also its force for evil. If it did not inform the mind, it at least did not absorb one's thoughts or turn them in other directions, toward competing ideas or creeds; and it could provide rest. Unlike poetry, music conveyed no heretical or immoral messages. Normally it brought before the mind's eye no wanton or lascivious pictures. Its appeal was purely aesthetic, and by accepting it, the puritans accepted art as form, unmixed with theological or moral elements. Poetry, on the other hand, had much greater potentialities for both good and evil. When acceptable, it was raised above the level of recreations and became a part of the necessary preparation for one's calling. When unacceptable, it was dangerous to the welfare of one's soul. Its content was representational; and when the content was good, the art gave it more force, more efficacy in impressing its message upon the reader or hearer. When the content was bad, art made it all the more dangerous by increasing its appeal. In neither case could poetry serve as mere recreation; it was too important, too closely connected with the general calling, if not with the particular.

---

[9] Whately, *Prototypes*, 46. For a study of the puritan acceptance of music, see Percy A. Scholes, *The Puritans and Music* (London: Oxford University Press, 1934).

The difference in puritan reception of the two closely related art forms is illustrated by one statement which is both exceptional and typical. In his *Guide to Godliness, or A Treatise of a Christian Life*, John Downame gave three chapters (Book III, Chapters 18, 19, 20) to the subject of callings, and typically his theory is almost a commentary on Perkins. In the three subsequent chapters, devoted to recreations, he gave an orthodox puritan statement of the lawful aims and varieties of sports. But unlike most puritans, he included poetry among the recreations, approving "the delighting of our minds . . . by using the excellent art of poetry, either making poems ourselves, or reading those which are composed by others." Yet the use of poetry required some further cautions, which are again typically puritan: "In all which, and the like exercises of the mind, our care must be that our recreations, neither in respect of words, matter, or manner, be wanton and wicked, insulse or corrupt, and neither bitter and biting, tending to the disgrace of others, nor profane and filthy." Immediately thereafter he achieved an orthodox perspective by naming music the highest of all recreations because it "above all other recreations is commended in the scriptures and by the example of the saints." For its use, no cautions are given, doubtless because none of the vices of poetry can be duplicated in music. [10]

Comparing the puritans' reception of music on the one hand and poetry on the other, we may infer that their aesthetic theory included a dichotomy between form and content. In fact, it has been shown that the New England puritans' acceptance of the Ramistic theory of rhetoric led them to consider art an embellishment of content, an addition of extrinsic ornaments to the logical core of meaning in written discourses. [11] The acceptance of music was thus an acceptance of art, as the puritans saw it, while the criticism of poetry showed an approval of the use of art to embellish moral discourses, but a condemnation of its use with vain or immoral content. In either case, the art itself was good, and a puritan could argue, as did Gosson, that he did not

[10] John Downame, *A Guide to Godlynesse* (1629), 266.
[11] Miller. *New England Mind*, 317.

condemn poetry itself even while he rejected poems of almost every variety. The dichotomy is widely present in English puritan writings, yet not universally so.

The variety of puritan opinion on the relationship of form and content can be illustrated by some comments on psalm translation and paraphrases. As part of Sacred Scripture, the psalms were the highest poetry. But they were Hebrew poetry, and when they were translated into English the question arose of reconciling exactness of translation with reproduction of artistic merits. Various puritans show clearly that in the translations they saw a clear distinction, even a conflict, between content and form. The problems and solutions of the translators were typically summarized by Baxter in a preface to his metrical paraphrase. Reflecting general opinion, he praises the "seraphic strain" of George Sandys but objects to his version mainly because it does not suit the usual tunes and so is not useful "to the vulgar." King's psalms are not ideal because of their unusual meter; like Sandys', King's version is good as poetry but fails didactically. Barton's version has failed in both ways; it is not effective because it is not sufficiently "grave." White's and Rowe's psalms are accurate translations, but not pleasing to the ear, whereas Woodford, Patrick, and Davison, in addition to Sandys, have been too free in translation. Baxter sums up the problem by giving his reasons for adding his own version to the multiplicity of existing texts: "I could not rest in the unpleasant harshness of the strictest versions, seeing psalms lose their ends that lose their affecting pleasure. I durst not venture on the paraphrastical liberty of others. . . . I feared adding to God's words . . . so that my labor hath been both to avoid the harshness and unpleasantness of strict versions, and the boldness of copious paraphrases." [12] By insisting upon the "affecting pleasure," Baxter apparently followed the Renaissance argument that literature had to profit by pleasing: the psychological assumption is the common one, used by preacher and poet, that the soul can be reached effectively mainly through the senses. Baxter was trying to harmonize what he saw as two distinct elements, the aes-

---

[12]Baxter, *Paraphrase on the Psalms of David*, preface.

thetic and the didactic. He thought both necessary, but he felt
that only with difficulty could they be made congruent.

Faced with the problem of achieving a balance, many puritans chose to risk erring on the side of literalness and harshness.
Some of these favored translations into English prose, while
others required of a metrical paraphrase no higher art than suitability to the usual simple tunes. Still others even perceived a
danger that in the singing itself the artistic element might inter-
fere with the didactic. For instance, Lewis Bayly warned his
readers to "beware of singing divine psalms for an ordinary
recreation," and to "be sure that the matter makes more melody
in your hearts, than the music in your ear." [13]

But a number of more sophisticated puritans could see no absolute distinction between the form and content of the psalms.
Because the psalms were Hebrew poems, they could be ade-
quately translated only if they were rendered as English poems,
for a prose paraphrase changed their nature and rendered them
only partially. John Cotton faced the artistic problem when he
argued for the practice of psalm singing. The translation of Hebrew songs into English songs he saw not only as a perfectly
legitimate act, but even as merely one aspect of the unquestionably laudable practice of translating Scripture into English. To
the objection that a metrical translation was a "poetical gift, not
a spiritual gift," he answers, "It might as well be said, the translating of the Hebrew Scripture into English is not a spiritual
gift but a grammatical or rhetorical gift. Whatsoever the art
or skill, grammatical, rhetorical, poetical, they are all of them
gifts of God (though common) and given chiefly for the service
and edification of the church of God." [14] Implicit here is a unified vision of all the aspects of the work as an integral whole.

The vision becomes explicit in the prefatory comments of
George Wither to his metrical paraphrases. Wither is characteristically puritan in his statement of aim to "write to the capacity
of the vulgar," and his claim that he has avoided "rhetorical illustrations" and "affected language." But he sees translation of

---

[13]Bayly, *Practice of Piety*, 312-13.
[14]John Cotton, *Singing of Psalmes A Gospel Ordinance* (1647), 56-57.

psalms as a practice entirely distinct from writing a mere paraphrase of meaning; adequate translation of psalms requires the preservation of a mood and tone inseparable from the meaning. Hence "the language of the muses in which the psalms were originally written, is not so properly expressed in the prose dialect as in verse." In fact, literal paraphrase may distort the meaning: "There is a poetical emphasis in many places, which requires such an alteration in the grammatical expression, as will seem to make some difference in the judgment of the common reader, whereas it giveth but life to the author's intention, and makes that perspicuous which was made obscure by those mere grammatical interpreters who were not acquainted with the proprieties and liberties of this kind of writing." And Wither practically erases the line between form and content when he expresses regard for "the censorious approbations of none, but such, as are (in their understanding at least) both divines and poets." [15] To Wither, poetic form and doctrinal meaning could not be understood separately; they were dimensions, not distinct elements, of a work of art.

Wither's approach to poetry thus differs from Baxter's, and his theory seems to be based on a radically different philosophy of art. But is it not possible that the relative degree of poetic sophistication accounts for the difference? Wither, as a poet by vocation, understood his theory; Baxter, as a minister and mere dabbler in poetry, did not have occasion to probe beneath the superficial, convenient distinctions of art and meaning to grasp the underlying unity. Baxter's theory served his purpose, to explain his choice of diction and meter. Cotton, trying to justify the metrical translation, had to go more deeply into literary theory and reached something of an organic view of the dimensions of a poem. Wither, approaching the question as a poet, easily penetrated superficial and irrelevant distinctions and worked directly from a basic theory in which form and content were inseparable. In any case, on the basis of Cotton's and Wither's statements, one an say that the puritans did not universally treat art as extrinsic to the substantial meaning of discourse.

---

[15] George Wither, *The Psalmes of David translated Into Lyrick-Verse* (1632), preface.

In their scattered and brief comments, the puritans do not appear to have been rigidly harsh critics of polite literature. If they were unduly strict, by modern standards, in their judging of recreations and, consequently, in their rejection of all forms of literature that served for popular amusements, their strictures derived less from an ascetic than from an aristocratic attitude. In this their specialized taste is akin to that of the twentieth-century critic who fails to perceive artistic merit in the cartoon or the cinema, and it does not distinguish them clearly from their contemporaries. Puritanism may have been antithetical to some types of humor and sophistication, but not to humanism or to devotion to the classics as they were then recognized. Many puritans esteemed the literary heritage of Greece or Rome as highly as did their contemporaries, and William Prynne, who was scarcely a libertine, gave his approval to the *Canterbury Tales* without a qualification. If most puritans were highly sensitive to the moral tendency of literary works, they were no less sensitive to literary artistry, and they readily quoted apt expressions from the very poets, such as Catullus, whom they condemned on moral grounds. The appreciation of rhetorical effects and graces of style showed itself also in their comments on their own writings, in which, in spite of their advocacy of a plain style as the best means to didactic ends, they apologized for lack of skill and often held up as the ideal quite traditional standards of human eloquence.

Of course, there were exceptions, but one can find a Thomas Taylor in movements much less comprehensive and heterogenous than puritanism. For one thing, every movement has its lunatic fringe. For another, the literary theory of the puritans was never systematized and distinguished from non-puritan theory, largely because the puritans never rebelled against the standard critical theory of their times. We find in their works a wide variety of attitudes taken from the Renaissance tradition and modified, by elaboration or shift of emphasis, in various ways and to various degrees. They achieved a high degree of uniformity when literature seemed to thwart their pragmatic concern to get the attention and time—ultimately the souls—of men, but even on polite literature the puritan ministers provided their adherents with a range of opinions from which they could choose without becoming unorthodox or losing sight of their ultimate goal of regeneration. Disagreements occurred even on the utility of plain style in a sermon and on the proper use of pagan quotations.

One is tempted to seek a pattern of variations, but it is difficult to trace. Although puritanism flourished during at least three-quarters of a century and marched under various banners at various times, its literary temper does not change in any distinct way with time. No clearly discernible literary principles or attitudes set off such early puritans as Greenham, Perkins, and Hieron as a group from such late puritans as Collinges, Reynolds, and Baxter; and in-between we find both Taylor and Gataker. Although puritanism embraced many varieties of ecclesiastical doctrine, now designated in general as Presbyterian, Independent, and Sectarian, with subdivisions that can be developed as long as one has the patience and the capacity to perceive distinctions, no crucial difference appears between the moderate, conforming Hieron, the Presbyterian Reynolds, and the staunchly independent John Goodwin.

The existing differences can be accounted for most easily on personal grounds. Generally, the specific context of a remark on literature conditioned the attitude it revealed; for the remarks were usually partial and relevant to the immediate situation. For instance, Hieron writing on the importance of preaching shows much less respect for written literature than Hieron trying to justify his verses against the "Popish" invader of his area. Also, the puritan, imbued with a specific didactic aim, was sensitive to the character of his audience. Whately, the preacher to an unsophisticated congregation at Danbury, found little use for pagan quotations and few occasions to commend polite literature, whereas preachers addressing Parliament showed no hesitation in citing and praising Greek and Roman literature. Yet, despite these conditioning circumstances, individual predispositions seem to have been most influential in determining the attitude of a minister toward polite literature. Gataker's works reveal a more intense interest in and a more profound response to the classics of the humanistic tradition than do those of his fellow London preachers, such as Gouge. Hieron's almost naive enjoyment of verse, Perkins' cautiously worded approval of poetry, Walwyn's enthusiasm for Montaigne, Taylor's distrustful glances at belles-lettres, Reynolds' eagerness to employ literature in the service of religion, Bolton's strangely inconsistent use of Catullus—all these seem highly personal phenomena, affected by education, experience, and temperament, undoubtedly, but not determined by political or religious affiliations. It follows, then, that instead of puritan literary theory we have a multiplicity of theories, and the foregoing chapters seem to indicate that the range of differences between puritan theories looms wider than the difference between the central theories of puritanism · and those of concurrent movements. Had puritanism been a doctrinaire religion, it might, because of its concern with the totality of human actions, have developed a systematic approach to literature; but as a general movement of church reform, whose members were united by opposition to the established church, it left literary criticism to the individual, passing beyond ecclesiastical questions only to the successive doctrinal and political problems with which the church in that age was inextricably involved. The general principles of union among the individual puritans did not give rigidity even to religious doctrine; much less could they impose uniformity in matters so extrinsic to religion as literature and art.

The puritans did take concerted action against the stage, but the stage as a social institution was attacked also by Giles Fletcher, John Marston, and numerous others, representing all shades of religious and political opinion. Significantly, Prynne was able to muster against it a list of authorities representing paganism, early Christianity, the medieval church, and then-contemporary Protestantism, including Anglicanism. Even then, the theatres were closed only with the advent of civil war; and if drama and other polite literature suffered after 1642, the civil conflict, open or simmering under the Commonwealth, must be largely to blame. The arts are generally not fostered by internecine strife; literary energies especially are channeled into more critical areas, such as ideological controversy. [16] The puritans deserve blame for the decline of the Elizabethan-Jacobean-Caroline tradition chiefly insofar as they were responsible for social and political upheavals. Their effect upon literature was thus incidental, and bore no necessary relation to their literary theories and attitudes. A band of literary zealots devoted to art for its own sake would, if it had precipitated a similar conflict, have had a like effect.

One other consideration may reduce still further the share of obloquy the puritans deserve for their at least indirect negative effect on literature. Partly they were merely the slaves or puppets of historical forces, and their attitudes, even toward popular literature, were molded by a determinism grounded in human nature, both individual and social. Although the Civil War did not occur by accident, it was not caused by the puritans or by the Anglicans, or by King or by Parliament. Among its multiple, complex causes, a major one was the reforming spirit itself, which, gaining impetus from the successes of Luther, Calvin, and their followers, could not rest in the Establishment. While it moved against no more than the force of tradition, which was elastic, though powerful, peaceful settlements were achieved. But when Laud gave the Establishment a counter-revolutionary dynamism, civil war was the only possible outcome, and we can, with three hundred years' hindsight, date the inevitability of armed conflict from his accession to power. Superficially, the puritans seem the aggressors, and in this sense they were aggressive also in their cautionary statements on literature. As exponents of a new order, they looked suspiciously at most of the phenomena accompanying the old. In their revolutionary zeal they tried to harness all their talents to the service of their idea. The confidence gained from precocious victories, in peace and later in war, merely seemed to justify more intense and single-minded efforts by bringing victory apparently within reach of a strenuous grasp. A belief, akin to that of the puritans, in the im-

---

[16] See Cowley's statement, in his preface to his *Works* (1668): "A warlike, various, and a tragical age is best to write of, but worst to write in." Abraham Cowley, *Poems*, ed. A. R. Waller (Cambridge: Cambridge University Press, 1905), 7.

minent establishment of a new utopia is vividly expressed in
some passages from the controversial writings of Milton—though
Milton always betrays some doubt about the ability of human
nature to achieve or merit utopia—where the call is always to
one more great effort. In this context, the puritan writers, who
looked upon themselves as literary men, felt the competition of
secular literature all the more keenly. Whether or not they
thought of Milton, we can take him as representative of their
ideal, insofar as he put aside his poetic plans to give his talents
to the puritan cause. Literature did suffer—how much we cannot know—but its main enemy was the single-mindedness
inherent in the revolutionary spirit, the single-mindedness which
shows itself boldly whenever the successful end of bitter conflict
seems within reach; the enemy was no definable principle in
whatever creed or philosophy distinguishes puritanism from
other revolutionary movements.

Would, then, the verdict of literary history upon the puritans
be different if they had established a durable hegemony over
church and state? The tentative answer is "yes," but ultimately
the question is pointless, for puritanism derived its principle
of union from a tendency, a tendency in a given direction with
no definite stopping point, as we can see now. The Presbyterians, by their insistence upon stopping at a new establishment,
alienated themselves from their former allies, so that civil unrest
continued after 1649, while the religious debate grew even more
acrimonious than it had been earlier. Puritanism, because of its
nature, could end only in defeat or enervation; either it had to
be overcome, or its energies had to be exhausted in bringing in a
new order. This is not to say that it was a negative movement,
but rather, that it was motivated by diverse and conflicting aims.
It could not establish itself as a new order; it could and did
prepare the way for the eventual settlement of 1688 by removing
the old order and so exhausting both puritans and Anglicans
that they were willing to accept a compromise far short of the
idealistic and irreconcilable aims that had led them into war.

The literary temper of the puritans, then, is heterogeneous, reflecting and incorporating various currents of non-puritan
thought. We should remember that in attacks on literature, in-

dividual puritans played disparate roles; we fall into an elementary error when, even by remote implication, we group Samuel How, Thomas Taylor, and Thomas Gataker under one general heading. The puritans are best treated in literary history as individuals, and when some of them, like Taylor, show a rather stringent asceticism in their attitudes toward literature, its genesis can most profitably be sought outside the puritan creed, philosophy, program, or ethos. Sometimes it can be found in the narrow pragmatism which some puritans shared with some non-puritan humanists and with many devotees of the new science. Sometimes it resides in an intellectual arrogance—from which humanists and Baconians were by no means free—that magnifies personal, private convictions and prejudices into cultural ideals. At any rate, to identify puritanism with literary obscurantism or with asceticism is to redefine the term until it no longer conveys the beliefs and attitudes of the men we think of as puritans. As it is commonly used in literary histories the word *puritan* may be somewhat convenient, but it is misleading; for it cannot be synchronized or made congruent—or even compatible—with the term *puritan* as it is applied in ecclesiastical or political history. Nor does it lead us to any generic impulses in the history of the seventeenth century, except indirectly, through the social and political history of the time. In other words, we can most profitably seek the change in the temper of seventeenth-century literature in a complex of religious, social, and political forces in which puritanism was only one element.

Index